Discover Loch Lomond &
The Trossachs National Park

Martin Varley has more than a decade's experience of working in conservation, including in national parks in both England and Scotland, and has previously written several successful books about the Lake District. He was Director of Friends of Loch Lomond & The Trossachs, a membership charity working to protect the landscape of Loch Lomond & The Trossachs National Park, between 2007 and 2009.

D1388741

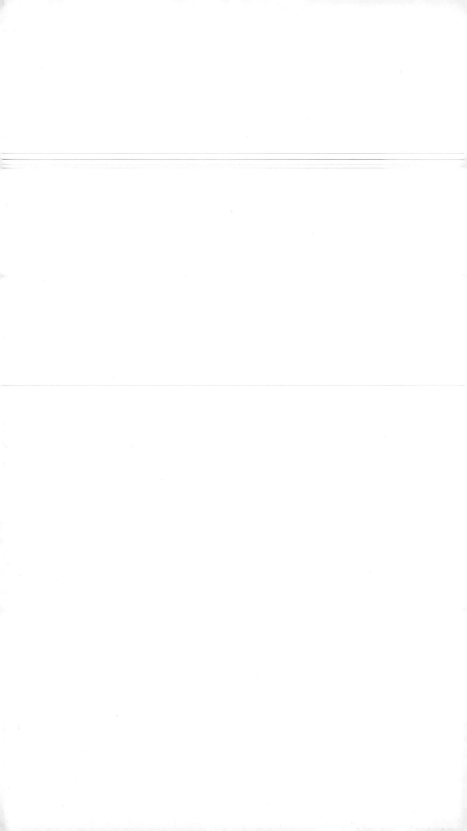

Discover Loch Lomond & The Trossachs National Park

Martin Varley

BIRLINN

friends OF LOCH LOMOND & THE TROSSACHS

First published in 2009 by
Birlinn Limited
West Newington House
10 Newington Road
Edinburgh
EH9 1QS

in association with
The Friends of Loch Lomond & The Trossachs National Park

www.birlinn.co.uk

ISBN: 978 1 84158 835 3

British Library Cataloguing-in-Publication Data
A catalogue record for this book is available from the British Library

This book has been sponsored by the
Loch Lomond & The Trossachs National Park Authority

Loch Lomond
& The Trossachs
National Park

Pàirc Nàiseanta Loch Laomainn
is nan Tròisichean

Typeset by Brinnoven, Livingston
Printed and bound by Bell & Bain Ltd, Glasgow

Contents

Key to Symbols Used

B&B	B&B/Hotel
SYHA	SYHA/Youth Hostel
△	Campsite
	Café/Restaurant/Pub
	Picnic places
i	Information centre
	Visitor attraction
	Shops
	Post Office
	Bank
P	Parking
WC	Toilets
	Boat cruises/trips
	Cycling
H	Bike hire
	Walking
	Sailing/watersports
H	Canoe/boat hire
	Fishing
	Telephone
	Hill walks

Opposite: Ben Lomond

PART ONE

INTRODUCTION

Loch Lomond & The
Trossachs National Park

Introduction

HISTORY

Long before people started measuring time, glaciers were shaping the landforms of Loch Lomond & The Trossachs National Park. When the ice finally retreated, around 12,000 years ago, its long, thin, cold fingers had scratched deep, narrow glens across the landscape. The weight of ice forced the land to sink and, before the land had time to recover, in rushed the sea, submerging the glens. Loch Lomond and Loch Eck were invaded by seawater and inhabited by marine fish and plants. The tides up the Lomond and Forth valleys nearly cut northern Scotland off from the rest of Britain, leaving plants and animals with a bridge of land only 10 miles wide over which to cross between the two.

The seas drew back as the land slowly rose and the landscape we see today began to take shape. The first colonisers clung to the freshly exposed rock: mosses, lichens and grasses coloured the bare soils. More adventurous low-growing shrubs followed, like dwarf birch and willow, crowberry and juniper. In their wake came migratory reindeer grazing across a tundra landscape resembling an ancient Lapland. Finally, in moved the forests. Tree varieties ebbed and flowed with the climate:

A row of giant redwood trees at Benmore Botanic Garden

first birch, then hazel, aspen, rowan, oak and Scots pine. None of that original woodland is around today. Once humans appeared on the scene the natural flow of ecological time was broken; the conifers of Argyll and Queen Elizabeth Forest Parks are immigrants of landscape history.

Prehistoric Times

People have lived in the National Park area since about 7000 BC. These first semi-nomadic hunter-gatherers left little behind to show us that they were here, apart from the odd flint axe-head. We need to fast-forward to the Bronze Age before we have any evidence of prehistoric life. Dunmore Fort, above Callander, Killin stone circle and the Puidrac standing stone in Balquhidder are all evidence of ancient human activity. But perhaps more significant are the crannogs – artificial islands built of boulders and timber piles onto which timber roundhouses could be built. These offered a defensible homestead with access to a wide range of resources. More than 20 have been uncovered in the park dating back to 500 BC, half of them on Loch Lomond.

The Highlands mark the furthest reaches of the Roman Empire. By the end of the first century invading forces were pushing north into Caledonia, the name the Romans gave to Scotland, and in particular the home of a Pictish tribe they called the Caledonii. Victory against the Caledonii warriors at Mons Graupius left Scotland at their mercy and the remains of Roman forts in the National Park date from this time: Drumquhassle, near Drymen; Malling, near Lake of Menteith; and Bochastle, near Callander. All were carefully positioned at the mouths of Highland glens, as if they were to be a springboard for a final conquest of the Highlands. But it never came; within a few years the forts were abandoned as the Roman legions left Scotland to fight battles closer to home.

The Dark Ages

After the Romans left, Scotland plunged into the Dark Ages. Details and timescales are sketchy, but by about AD 600 the mountains around Loch Lomond were thought to have formed a frontier between the three dominant kingdoms which eventually emerged out of tribal chaos following the departure of the Romans. To the south were the Britons whose territory stretched from Loch Lomond south towards Carlisle. In the west were Celtic Gaels who had come over from Ireland. They had conquered the land we now call Argyll and renamed it Dalriada. The Romans called them Scotii and their descendants would eventually give their name to the whole country. Finally, to the north-east stretched the kingdom of the Picts. Tradition maintains that the three kingdoms met at the Clach nam Breatann (the Stone of the Britons) which still stands on a hillside in Glen Falloch. Another stone, Clach a' Breatannaich, near Lochgoilhead, was said to mark the boundary between the Britons and the Scotii.

The National Park area was a land of tensions as the three tribes clashed with one another. It was the coming of Christianity which helped to unify these disparate groups after Celtic missionaries began to arrive in the sixth century. St Kessog came to Luss, on the shores of Loch Lomond; St Kentigerna set up a church on Inchcailloch; St Mun is remembered at Holy Loch and Kilmun, in Argyll; St Fillan worked throughout Breadalbane; and St Angus preached in Balquhidder. The influence of the churches which they established remained long after the saints had gone. By AD 1300 there were a dozen parish churches in the National Park area whose roots reached back to the early saints. Most of them are still in use today and though the churches themselves have been rebuilt, some medieval remains can still be seen.

Dundurn Hill Fort dates back to the eighth century

Calm waters on Loch Lomond

While missionaries changed the culture, successive kings moved the politics and in AD 843 Kenneth MacAlpine finally united Dalriada and Pictland. The Picts traced succession through the female line and MacAlpine used his influence as a Dalriadic king and his inheritance as the son of a Pictish princess to create the kingdom of Alba. It would later become Scotia and ultimately Scotland.

The Coming of the Clans

Sitting on the boundary between the Highlands and the Lowlands, the political history of Scotland, and in particular the role of the clans, has helped to shape the cultural landscape of the National Park. Clans – closely knit territorial groups of related people, often families with a chief – first emerged in the twelfth and thirteenth centuries and local history resonates with names like Campbell, MacGregor, MacFarlane, Colquhoun and MacNab. Characterised by tragedy and treachery, their stories are always colourful, often bloody and never dull.

Rob Roy MacGregor is perhaps the best-known figure from this time, having roamed across the lands of Loch Lomond, the Trossachs and Balquhidder Glen in the late seventeenth and early eighteenth centuries. But there are others whose memory echoes through the land.

One legacy of the clans is their castles – seats and strongholds which symbolise their power. They were the pride of the defender and the prize of the aggressor in the clan battles of the past. Yet now most are in ruins and neglected, their stories remaining untold, the importance of their historic role unknown. Of the 30 or so medieval stone castles and towers found in the National Park today only three are occupied and three others have been incorporated into newer buildings. Most are ivy-covered, roofless ruins, abandoned shells whose stone has been robbed for walled gardens and farm buildings.

The clans fell with the failed Jacobite rebellions of the eighteenth century, when those who supported the Catholic House of Stuart fought and lost to the ruling Protestant House of Hanover. The majority of Highlanders were loyal to the Stuarts, while the neighbouring Lowlanders sided with the Hanovarians, although boundaries were often blurred. When Bonnie Prince Charlie was defeated at the Battle of Culloden in 1746, those who had sided with him were harshly dealt with. At worst they were executed and at best they had their lands taken from them.

Cottages at Luss

After that the face of the National Park landscape changed forever as government generals planned for a future where there would be no room for future uprisings. In 1724 General Wade had been sent to Scotland and had recommended the construction of barracks, bridges and proper roads to assist in the policing of the region. In the National Park, his successor Major Caulfeild created quadrants of control with his road-building programme. In the east he built a road from Callander to Killin and along Glen Dochart to Crianlarich. His road along the west side of Loch Lomond split at Tarbet with one arm going over to Loch Long and Inveraray and the other travelling north to Fort William. Many of the park's roads today follow the same lines as these old military roads.

The Tourist Era

The Loch Lomond and the Trossachs area has long been admired by visitors. No sooner had the clans gone than the crowds arrived. Sir Walter Scott's reinvention of the Trossachs as a must-see tourist destination through his Romantic writings happened less than a generation after the death of the area's most famous clansman, Rob Roy MacGregor. Although the celebrated Dr Johnson described Loch Lomond's scenery as 'uncultivated ruggedness' when he passed through on his journey to the Western Islands of Scotland in 1773, those who followed in his footsteps were more appreciative of its natural beauty. Dorothy and William Wordsworth, Samuel Taylor Coleridge, Queen Victoria, Hans Christian Andersen, Jules Verne and Thomas Cook are among the list of famous travellers who have waxed lyrical about the area's scenic appeal.

However, with the majority of Scotland's population less than an hour from the area, it is the masses that have truly shaped tourism here. From the Victorian era onwards, carriages, coaches, trains, steamers and cars have brought people here to walk, climb, sail, fish, cycle, horse-ride or just watch the landscape go by. Such pressure for recreation and access did not come without its price as tourism development threatened the very landscape which people wanted to see. As early as the 1930s guidebook writers were expressing the need for the protection of Loch Lomond.

In 1978 this recognition led to the creation of the Friends of Loch Lomond, whose aim was to ensure that the natural beauty of the area was safeguarded, at a time when others only talked about it. But the organisation was voluntary. Despite John Muir, the father of national parks, being a Scotsman, and his efforts to protect America's wilderness leading to the creation of Yosemite National Park in 1890, it was over a century later in 2002 that Loch Lomond and the Trossachs area became Scotland's first national park. Although the two areas from which

The Scotch argus butterfly is part of the National Park's diverse wildlife

the park takes it name are the most popular for visitors, the National Park is divided into four distinct areas: Loch Lomond, the Trossachs, Breadalbane and the Argyll Forest, each with its own character and individual appeal.

Unlike many national parks in the world, Loch Lomond & The Trossachs National Park is not owned by the government, but is a living, working landscape. Over 15,000 people live inside the park, mostly in the south and east, and the countryside is owned by individual farmers and landowners. The Loch Lomond & The Trossachs National Park Authority is a government body responsible for conserving the natural beauty and cultural heritage of the area whilst supporting the social and economic wellbeing of local communities. It is also the planning authority for the local communities and has its headquarters in Balloch. Tourism is the main source of employment with between two and three million people visiting the area each year. Agriculture and forestry are also important.

Highland Boundary Fault

The Highland Boundary Fault, sometimes called the Highland Line, marks the division between the Highlands and the Lowlands. Geologically it splits Scotland in two and it has helped to shape the nation culturally too. North of the faultline the landscape is rugged and mountainous, home of the highest peaks in the British Isles and the worst weather.

To the south and east the landscape is softer, agriculture is easier and the weather is more temperate. This contrast has seeped into Scotland's history. In the past, the clan system with its chieftains developed in the Highlands while the feudal system established by the kings of Scotland and their lairds developed in the Lowlands; dress was different, as were architecture, language and even travel. Ultimately this division resulted in conflict between the Highland clans and their wealthier Lowland neighbours, exacerbated by the Jacobite rebellions and the Highland Clearances. And even today the contrast is marked by the prevalence of the Gaelic language in the Highlands.

The Highland Boundary Fault traverses Scotland from Arran and Helensburgh in the west to Stonehaven in the east and scores a line across the landscape of the southern half of the National Park as it passes. The contrast between the Highlands and Lowlands bequeathed to us by the fault is a recurring feature in the park. The best places to see evidence of the fault are at Conic Hill, Balmaha and on the Highland Boundary Fault Trail at the David Marshall Lodge, Aberfoyle.

MUNROS

Munros are distinctly Scottish mountains which have a height of over 3,000 feet (914.4 metres). They are named after Sir Hugh Munro (1856–1919), who produced the first compilation of a catalogue of such hills, known as *Munro's Tables*, in 1891. There are 284 Munros in Scotland and the challenge of climbing all of them is a popular pursuit for many hillwalkers. The National Park has 21 Munros mostly in the north and west, including Scotland's most southerly Munro, Ben Lomond.

Climbing a Munro is not an activity to be taken lightly. Munros are often in remote locations where finding your way may be difficult. Conditions on their summits can be bleak: the fall in temperature from the Rowardennan car park to the top of Ben Lomond can be as much as 7°C. With added wind chill it is easy to see why Munros can have a climate more like the Arctic than the Atlantic. Always go out suitably prepared if attempting to climb a Munro. The Scottish Mountaineering Club (www.smc.org.uk) has more information about Munros and hillwalking.

Munros in the National Park and the closest village:

An Caisteal (995 m), Crianlarich

Beinn a' Chroin (940 m), Crianlarich

Beinn a' Chleibh (916 m), Tyndrum

Beinn Ime (1,011 m), Arrochar

Ben Chabhair (933 m), Ardlui

Ben Challuim (1,025 m), Tyndrum

Ben Dubhcraig (978 m), Tyndrum

Ben Lomond (974 m), Balmaha

Ben Lui (1,130 m), Tyndrum

Ben More (1,174 m), Crianlarich

Beinn Narnain (926 m), Arrochar

Ben Oss (1,029 m), Tyndrum

Ben Tulaichean (945 m), Crianlarich

Ben Vane (915 m), Ardlui

Ben Vorlich (by Loch Earn) (985 m), Lochearnhead

Ben Vorlich (by Loch Lomond) (943 m), Ardlui

Cruach Ardrain (1,046 m), Crianlarich

Meall Glas (959 m), Crianlarich

Sgiath Chuil (921 m), Crianlarich

Stob Binnein (1,165 m), Crianlarich

Stuc a' Chroin (975 m), Lochearnhead

Mountain avens

Access to land and water in the National Park is guided by the Scottish Outdoor Access Code. Under the code everyone has the right to be on most land and inland water providing they act responsibly. Put simply, individuals should take responsibility for their own actions, respect the interests of other people and care for the environment. For more information on the code visit www.outdooraccess-scotland.com.

FRIENDS OF LOCH LOMOND & THE TROSSACHS

Friends of Loch Lomond & The Trossachs is a conservation charity which works across the National Park to safeguard the area's natural beauty and cultural heritage. Its members are passionate about keeping Scotland's first national park a special place. To find out more about the society, its work and how to join, visit www.lochlomondtrossachs. org.uk.

WHEN TO GO

The National Park experiences less of a climate and more of a random series of weather events. There can be four seasons in the same place in one day, or four seasons in four places at the same time. The old idiom of if you don't like the weather just wait a few minutes or travel a few miles holds good here and is part of the enjoyment of a visit. Charles Dickens had the right attitude to the park's fickle climate in his description of the area in 1841: 'This is a wondrous region. The way the mists were stalking about today, and the clouds lying down upon the hills, the high rocks, the rushing waterfalls and roaring rivers down in deep gulfs below were all stupendous.'

The National Park holds the dubious accolade of receiving the heaviest rainfall period ever recorded in Scotland. In January 1974, more than the entire month's average rainfall fell in a single day – 238.4 mm at Loch Sloy in the Arrochar Alps. The park's proximity to Scotland's west coast makes it the first area to be hit by weather systems sweeping in with rain from the Atlantic. Rainfall is greater in winter than summer and more falls in the north and west than south and east. Visitors to the area for more than a few days would be wise to prepare for rain at some point.

The park's westerly location also makes it very mild – the Cowal peninsula is sufficiently balmy for palm trees to grow. Despite being at the same latitude as Moscow, the park has nothing like the extremes of temperature experienced in central Russia, typically 14.5°C in July and 4.5°C in December. Winters tend not to be too cold and snow is

Evening light on Loch Lomond

seldom a problem on lower ground. The last time the southern half of Loch Lomond completely froze over was more than 50 years ago, in 1963. With global warming it seems unlikely that it will happen again in the next 50 years.

The warmest months are July and August, which are also the worst months for the scourge of the Highlands: the midge. Many creams and potions have been developed to counter the invasion of this irritating insect. It would be worth carrying at least one variety of repellent or a midge-net hat if considering visiting during the summer months, particularly if camping. However, the park's northerly latitude does offer compensation in the summer when the long days make it feel like the sun never sets and an extended twilight descends upon the landscape.

Although not the hottest months, spring and autumn are good times to visit the National Park. These months are still warm and not as wet as at other times. The park comes alive with wildlife in spring and in autumn the changing colours of the leaves grace the trees. There is plenty of room in the National Park and it is possible to find solitude even at the busiest times. But if you enjoy peace and quiet then winter can be a good time to come. However, bear in mind that many tourist attractions and businesses are closed during the quieter periods.

Getting There and Getting Around

By plane: Glasgow is the closest international airport to the National Park. Edinburgh also has an international airport and there are good transport links between the two cities. Buses run regularly from Glasgow Airport to Paisley railway station, where there are connections to Glasgow Central station from where public transport to the National Park departs. A bus service transfers passengers between Glasgow Central and Glasgow Queen Street stations or Buchanan bus station every 10 minutes.

By train: Travel to the west side of the National Park by taking a train to the station at Balloch and then a connecting bus, or by getting off at one of the stations along the West Highland Railway. There are stops at Arrochar and Tarbet, Ardlui, Crianlarich and Tyndrum. To get to the east side of the National Park take a train to Stirling and get a bus from there. Trains for each destination depart from Glasgow Queen Street station.

By bus: Buses from Glasgow to the National Park depart from Buchanan bus station and go direct to Balloch and further stops on the A82. Bus services in the National Park are operated by a number of providers. Services run between most of the villages, but it is best to check times locally. Where a bus service runs to a location in this guide it is indicated in the relevant section.

The Loch Lomond 4Bs service runs during the summer between Balloch and Tarbet. This service has capacity for carrying bikes and is timetabled to link with Loch Lomond ferry services. For more information visit www.lochlomond4bs.co.uk.

The Trossachs Trundler is a summer bus service following a circular route through the Trossachs which links Callander, Port of Menteith and Aberfoyle. It also calls at Loch Katrine, where it is timed to connect with the sailings of the ss *Sir Walter Scott*. It is wheelchair-accessible and fitted with a bike rack for two bikes. Reasonable luggage space is available for rucksacks.

For further information on getting to and getting around the National Park contact Traveline Scotland on 📞 0871 200 22 33 or visit www.travelinescotland.com. Alternatively get hold of a copy of the public transport booklet *Exploring the National Park by Ferry, Bus and Train* from tourism information centres or download it from www.lochlomond-trossachs.org.

By boat: The following operators run cruises in the National Park: *Cruise Loch Lomond Ltd* – all-year-round cruises based in Tarbet 📞 01301 702356; www.cruiselochlomondltd.com

Inversnaid Hotel runs a ferry between Inveruglas and Inversnaid 📞 01877 386223

Macfarlane & Son Boatyard – cruises to Inchcailloch and Inchmurrin from Balmaha 📞 01360 870214

Mullens Cruises – cruises on Loch Lomond from Balloch 📞 01389 751481

Loch Lomond Ferry Service operates between Rowardennan to Inverbeg daily, April to September 📞 01360 870273

Loch Katrine Experience – cruises on Loch Katrine aboard a Victorian passenger steamer 📞 01877 332000; www.lochkatrine.com

Sweeney's Cruises – cruises on Loch Lomond from Balloch: 📞 01389 752376; www.sweeney.uk.com

Inchmurrin Island ferry – ferry from Midross: 📞 01389 850245; www.inchmurrin-lochlomond.com

By bike: There are numerous opportunities for cycling in the National Park. National Cycle Route 7 begins at Dumbarton and passes through Balloch, Drymen, Aberfoyle, Callander and Killin. Regional Cycle Route 40 runs up the west side of Loch Lomond (A leaflet on the West Loch Lomond Cycle Path and a leaflet describing a selection of cycling routes in the National Park can be downloaded from www.lochlomond-trossachs.org). The Forestry Commission Scotland has designed off-road cycle routes around its sites at Loch Ard, Achray Forest, Glenbranter and Ardgartan. For more details 📞 01877 382383 or visit www.forestry.gov.uk/scotland. More information on cycle hire centres is given in relevant chapters.

INFORMATION, MAPS AND BOOKS

A range of information on the National Park is available. The National Park Authority's website (www.lochlomond-trossachs.org) is a good place to start. The Forestry Commission Scotland owns large parts of the National Park and also has information on its website (www.forestry.gov.uk/scotland).

Although walks are detailed in this guide, they are descriptive and an appropriate map should always be used. The National Park is covered by Ordnance Survey (www.ordnancesurvey.co.uk) at both 1:50,000 scale (Landranger maps 56 and 57) and 1:25,000 scale (Explorer maps 347, 363, 364 and 365). Harvey (www.harveymaps.co.uk) produces 1:25,000 scale hillwalkers maps of Crianlarich, Ben Venue, the Arrochar Alps, Ben Lomond and Ben Ledi, as well as a 1:40,000 scale spiral-bound atlas of the whole National Park. For an easy-to-use map of the entire

Information centres in and around the National Park:

National Park

Loch Lomond Shores, Balloch 📞 0845 345 4978
Balmaha 📞 01389 722100
Luss 📞 01389 722120

VisitScotland

Aberfoyle Open all year 📞 08707 200604
Ardgartan Open Easter to October 📞 08707 200606
Balloch Open all year 📞 08707 200607
Callander Open all year 📞 08707 200628
Dumbarton Open Easter to October 📞 08707 200612
Dunoon Open all year 📞 08707 200629
Helensburgh Open Easter to October 📞 08707 200615
Killin Open all year 📞 08707 200627
Stirling Open all year 📞 08707 200620
Tarbet Open Easter to October 📞 08707 200623
Tyndrum Open all year 📞 08707 200626

Canoeing on Loch Lomond

National Park, Footprint (www.footprintmaps.co.uk) produces a useful combined tourist map and guide.

Although much has been written about individual parts of the National Park, there are few books which cover the whole area. Two accessible books which explore the history of the Loch Lomond and the Trossachs region are *The Trossachs – History and Guide* by William F. Hendrie (Tempus) and *Loch Lomond and the Trossachs in History and Legend* by P.J.G. Ransom (Birlinn). John Barrington has written an interesting A–Z gazetteer on the National Park in his book *Loch Lomond and The Trossachs* (Luath Press).

For books on specific areas of the park, the New Naturalist Series guide *Loch Lomondside* by John Mitchell (HarperCollins) is a learned account of the natural history of the loch and its surroundings. A more general descriptive introduction to this area is given by Stewart Noble in his *By the Banks of Loch Lomond* (Argyll Publishing). In the north of the park, *The Braes o' Balquhidder* by Elizabeth Beauchamp (Friends of Balquhidder Church) is a readable account of the history of that glen and *In Famed Breadalbane* by Rev. William A. Gillies (Northern Books) is a reprint of a scholarly account of the lands and lairds of Glen Dochart, Strathfillan and the surrounding area, first published in 1938. To dig deeper into the area's history get hold of *Rob Roy MacGregor: His Life and Times* by W.H. Murray (Canongate), the biography on which the 1995 film of his life was based. To explore more about the

Walkers on the West Highland Way

clans try Fitzroy Maclean's *Highlanders: A History of the Scottish Clans* (Overlook Press).

For walking enthusiasts, the Scottish Mountaineering Club's guide to *The Southern Highlands* is a classic descriptive guide and covers walks and climbs in the National Park. For a more contemporary guide try Ronald Turnbull's *Walking Loch Lomond and the Trossachs* (Cicerone Press), *25 Walks: Loch Lomond and the Trossachs* by Roger Smith and John Digney (Mercat Press) or *Loch Lomond & The Trossachs National Park* Vol. 1 & Vol. 2 by Tom Prentice (Mica Press). Footprint also produces a range of inexpensive maps and guides to walking and cycling in parts of the National Park. For the West Highland Way, Bob Aitken and Roger Smith have written *The West Highland Way: The Official Guide* (Mercat Press) and Jacquetta Megarry has written *The Rob Roy Way* (Rucksack Readers), a map and guide covering the sections of this long-distance route which fall within the National Park.

ACCOMMODATION, FOOD AND DRINK

There is no detailed information on accommodation included in this guide, but there are plenty of places where this type of information is readily available particularly on the internet and at information centres. Instead this guide focuses primarily on discovering the natural and cultural history – what there is to do and where to go – in Scotland's first national park. Individual sections do mention whether local accommodation is available, but specific details are omitted. There are many places to stay in the National Park ranging from simple campsites to exclusive hotels, so there is something to suit everyone and every pocket. Many local businesses, towns, villages and regions have their own websites, often offering information on accommodation. These are included in this guide where possible. You can also book accommodation at VisitScotland information centres in the National Park.

If you are staying in the area, look out for businesses which are members of the Green Tourism Business Scheme. This scheme requires businesses to fulfil certain environmental sustainability criteria, so you can have confidence that the impact on the environment of your stay will be minimised. If you are not sure whether a business is in the scheme, ask, or visit www.green-business.co.uk for a list of members in the National Park area.

There are plenty of places to eat in the National Park. Locations with cafés and restaurants are marked in the guide. Tourism is the main industry of the National Park and many businesses depend upon visitors spending time in the area and using local services. If you are able to shop locally during your visit not only will this enhance your enjoyment of the National Park by exploring what these shops and services have to offer, but you will also be helping the local economy.

FESTIVALS, SHOWS AND ANNUAL EVENTS

Distinctive local celebrations are among the highlights of the year in the National Park, and most of them take place during the summer and autumn. Traditional Highland games are held at a number of venues. These are a celebration of Highland culture, so expect kilts, bagpipes, caber-tossing, piping, drumming and dancing as well as other entertainment relating to clan traditions. There are also agricultural shows, and music, arts, walking and outdoor festivals which have become fixtures in the annual events calendar.

The National Park Authority runs an events programme each year. Pick up an events guide at an information centre or visit www.lochlomond-trossachs.org. You can also give your time as a volunteer in the National Park, getting involved in practical conservation tasks, surveys and helping at events. The Forestry Commission Scotland offers a programme of events too, on its sites in the Argyll Forest and Queen Elizabeth Forest Parks. Again, pick up a guide or visit www.forestry.gov.uk/scotland for more information. Information centres should also be able to provide details of what's going on in the area.

Highland games, events and festivals in the National Park:

March

Argyll Classic Car Run – an annual classic car event which passes through the National Park, organised by the Caledonian Classic and Historic Motorsport Club (www.caledonianmsc.freeuk.com)

Tramping through the Trossachs – events and activities celebrating the great outdoors (www.visitaberfoyle.com)

May

The Drymen Show – a traditional agricultural show (www.drymenshow.com)

Bluebell Festival – a celebration of spring (www.forestry.gov.uk/scotland)

July

Loch Lomond Highland Games, Balloch (www.loch-lomond-highland-games.com)

Loch Lomond Folk Festival, Balloch (www.lomondfolkfestival.com)

A traditional parade at the Killin Games

Lochearnhead Highland Games
(www.lochearnheadhighlandgames.co.uk)

Rob Roy Highland Games, Strathard

Callander World Highland Games (www.incallander.co.uk)

Luss Highland Gathering (www.lusshighlandgames.co.uk)

Killin International Highland Games (www.killingames.co.uk)

National Parks Week – events and activities celebrating
national parks.

August

Killin and District Agricultural Show – a traditional
agricultural show

Cowal Highland Gathering, Dunoon (www.cowalgathering.com)

Balquhidder Summer Music Festival – a series of classical music
concerts held in Balquhidder Church

Clanscape, Killin – a festival of traditional activities with a
Highland theme

Cultural events take place across the National Park

September

Breadalbane Arts Week

Loch Lomond Food and Drink Festival at Loch Lomond Shores (www.lochlomondshores.com)

October

Cowalfest – outdoor activities and art festival with events throughout the Cowal peninsula (www.cowalfest.org)

Callander Jazz and Blues Festival – a long weekend of live jazz and blues music in the Trossachs (www.callanderjazz.info)

Crieff and Strathearn Drovers' Tryst – a celebration of the traditions of the drovers (www.droverstryst.co.uk)

Aberfoyle International Mushroom Festival – an autumnal celebration of edible fungi; includes woodland walks (www.visitaberfoyle.com)

Cyclists taking part in the Cowalfest, held in October

Opposite: Falls of Falloch

PART TWO

LOCH LOMOND

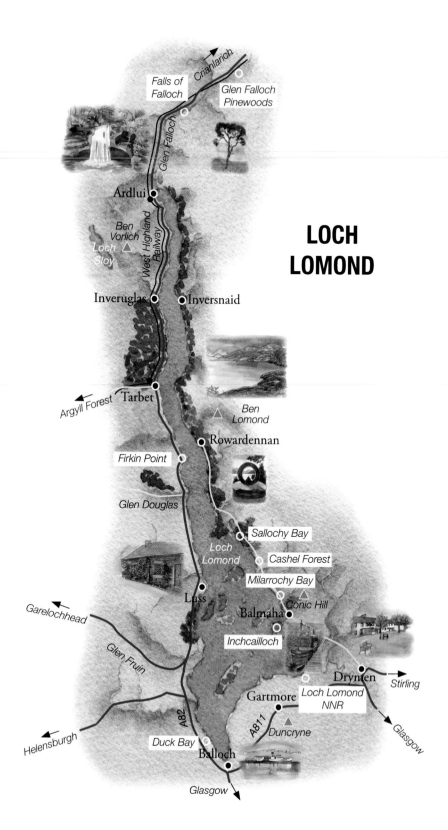

LOCH LOMOND

Crianlarich

Falls of Falloch

Glen Falloch Pinewoods

Glen Falloch

Ardlui

Ben Vorlich

Loch Sloy

West Highland Railway

Inveruglas

Inversnaid

Argyll Forest

Tarbet

Ben Lomond

Rowardennan

Firkin Point

Glen Douglas

Sallochy Bay

Loch Lomond

Cashel Forest

Milarrochy Bay

Garelochhead

Luss

Balmaha

Conic Hill

Glen Fruin

Inchcailloch

Drymen

Stirling

Gartmore

Loch Lomond NNR

A82

Glasgow

A811

Duncryne

Helensburgh

Duck Bay

Balloch

Glasgow

Loch Lomond

Panorama of Loch Lomond

Even the most tuneless among us can probably hum along to 'The Bonnie Banks o' Loch Lomond'. First published in 1841 and recorded by artists ranging from Bill Haley and the Comets to the Band of the Coldstream Guard, it is one of Scotland's most enduring anthems. The 'Bonnie Banks o' Loch Lomond' is thought to have been written by a Jacobite prisoner during the uprising of 1745, but the subject of his lament came into being long before Highlanders and Lowlanders fought over this land, when a glacier flowing south from the Highlands gouged out the loch. At 24 miles long, and 5 miles wide at its southern end, it contains the largest volume of freshwater in the UK. Its northern reaches plunge to depths deeper than the North Sea. The glacier also left behind Ben Lomond. One translation of the name of is 'the Hill of Fire', and in the past warning beacons were lit from its summit. It certainly acts as a beacon today, drawing thousands of people to climb it each year.

At the end of the last ice age Loch Lomond was inundated by the sea and only gradually reverted to a freshwater loch. The powan – a rare fish related to salmon – adapted to this change and is now only found here and in Loch Eck. This seldom-seen celebrity is not alone. Loch Lomond has more species of fish than any other loch: salmon and trout, pike and perch, roach and minnows, sticklebacks, lampreys and eels swim in its waters. It is not only fish that occur in profusion: a quarter of all UK flowering plants can be found here too and there are over 200 species of birds from the charismatic capercaillie to the commonplace chaffinch. Its woodlands of oak, birch and alder, carpeted with bluebells in the spring and coloured with gold in the autumn, are among Scotland's greatest natural glories.

Less than 30 miles from Glasgow, it is not surprising that Loch Lomond is a favourite destination for day-trippers from the city, carrying on a connection which goes back to the Industrial Revolution. Then, many of the towns around the loch developed to supply Glasgow with raw materials of stone, wood and water for its growth. Now fresh air and freedom are the area's most valuable commodities.

BALLOCH

Buses connect Balloch with Glasgow, Drymen, Balmaha, west Loch Lomond
Trains connect Balloch with Glasgow
Information centre 📞 08707 200607; **www.visit-balloch.com**

Balloch has long been a village of transition, caught between the city and the countryside. To the north lie the open waters of Loch Lomond and wilder moors of the National Park's mountains, to the south a ribbon of settlements snakes down the Vale of Leven towards the river Clyde and on to Glasgow. The Vale of Leven can claim to be the birthplace of the textile industry in Scotland, as the first recorded bleachfields were at Dalquhurn, 2 miles south of Balloch. After being washed in nearby streams, linen cloth was laid out on bleachfields to be whitened in the sun. The 1707 Treaty of Union between Scotland and England had opened up new markets in the English colonies and Glasgow merchants were ideally placed to exploit the Atlantic routes with all the necessary raw materials close at hand.

The Highland Clearances of the eighteenth century, although devastating further north, coincided with this rise of the local textile industry. Displaced workers from the countryside were soaked up by the spinning, weaving and cloth-printing industries. Villages like Balloch took advantage of the power of the fast-flowing rivers of soft water that was needed for both dyeing and bleaching. By the turn of the nineteenth century there were five bleachfields and six printworks along a short stretch of the river Leven south of Balloch, employing 3,000 men, women and children.

However, the boom was short-lived and within a century the industry was already struggling to overcome increased competition from abroad and from south of the border. The last textile works closed in 1960. Nowadays, Balloch relies upon another of its traditional industries and is a major tourism centre for the National Park, as it has been for 200 years. Back then visitors like Dorothy Wordsworth would take a steamboat from Glasgow to Dumbarton, followed by a coach to Balloch, before embarking on a cruise on the loch. In her diary of 1822 she recalled that the waves were 'so large we might have fancied ourselves at sea'. By 1850 the railway had arrived, allowing day-trippers direct access from Glasgow, as they still have today.

Many more modern visitors come by road, although the route is quieter than it once was as the A82 now bypasses much of the Vale of Leven on its way up the western side of the loch. Balloch's importance as a gateway to the National Park is reinforced by the presence of the headquarters of the National Park Authority in the centre of the village. The building is worth a mention in its own right as a modern example of a sustainable building. Built of slate and timber and using natural light and biomass heating, it boasts a 70 per cent reduction in carbon footprint compared to a conventionally designed office and acts as a model for similar buildings in the twenty-first century.

Balloch town centre lies to the north of the A811 along the parallel Balloch Road. At the western end of Balloch Road, a road leads off to **Loch Lomond Shores**. Half-hourly trains run to Glasgow Queen Street

The River Leven at Balloch

from the railway station, which is centrally located opposite the visitor information centre. The road crosses the river Leven, where loch cruises start and a footpath runs to the loch shore and the *Maid of the Loch* paddle steamer. Buses for Glasgow, Oban and local services east and west of the loch leave from a turning area on the eastern side of the river opposite the entrance to the **Balloch Castle Country Park**. There is parking at Loch Lomond Shores and in the centre of Balloch.

THE LOCH SHORE

Information centre 📞 0845 345 4978

The main visitor attraction on the loch shore is **Loch Lomond Shores** (📞 01389 751035, www.lochlomondshores.com) a development which includes a traditional shopping centre, plus a few extras, set against the background of the loch. The main complex is a curving crescent of shops and cafés which contour the shoreline. Standing sentinel alongside the shops is the **Loch Lomond Aquarium** (📞 0871 423 2110), occupying the turret-like Drumkinnon Tower. Using the waters of the National Park as its theme, the aquarium takes visitors on a journey starting at the Falls of Falloch, moving through Loch Lomond and on to the Clyde estuary. You can hire bikes and canoes (📞 01389 602576; www. canyouexperience.com) or enjoy a family walk in nearby woodlands. Also nearby is the **National Park Gateway Centre**, with exhibitions and interactive displays about the National Park and information about where to go and what to do.

For boat launching on the loch, head for the **Duncan Mills Memorial Slipway** (📞 01389 757295), a ranger base with parking and public boat-launch and registration facilities. Adjacent to the slipway is moored the *Maid of the Loch* paddle steamer (📞 01389 711865; www.maidoftheloch. com). Steamer services have long been associated with the loch, ever since the *Marion* first plied the waters in 1818. Successive steamers sailed Loch Lomond until the 1980s. The *Maid of the Loch* was the last paddle steamer built in Britain. In 2004, she officially became an historic ship, being placed on the UK Designated Vessels List which recognises vessels of 'substantial heritage merit' and 'regional and local significance'. Efforts are now under way to restore the vessel and return her to steam operation on the loch. You can still pay her a visit and there is a café and gift shop on board.

BALLOCH CASTLE COUNTRY PARK

Abutting the bonny, bonny banks of Loch Lomond, Balloch Castle Country Park offers woodland and lochside walks, and a nature trail. The area was originally developed in the early nineteenth century by John Buchanan, a partner in the Glasgow Ship Bank. It was purchased by Glasgow City Corporation in 1915 in response to the needs of the ever increasing number of visitors to the area and went on to become Scotland's first country park. The centrepiece of the park is Balloch Castle, which Buchanan built using stone from the original castle built in 1238 by the Lennox family and occupied until about 1390. The only remnant of the original structure is a mound that once formed part of the moat.

Balloch Castle Country Park

The Eastern Shore

Starting out from Balloch there are really only two routes available to explore Loch Lomond, either along its eastern shore or its western shore. For many the eastern shore is the heart of Loch Lomond. The western shoreline is hugged by the A82, a road which transports people as fast as possible past the loch, often to a destination far beyond the National Park. However, a journey along the eastern shore is a more intimate encounter with the landscape, slower and with only the loch as your destination.

From Drymen the narrow shore-side road covers only 15 miles of the loch's full 24-mile length. After Balmaha there are countless spots where the loch surprises, with new views appearing between the trees or around corners, until its end at Rowardennan. Fittingly the road comes to rest at the foot of the guardian of Loch Lomond, Ben Lomond, whose shoulders rise out of the water signifying the start of the Highlands. From here the only way north to Inversnaid and beyond is on foot, following Rob Roy, Robert the Bruce and countless anonymous travellers along the lochside route popularised by the West Highland Way.

GARTOCHARN

Buses connect Gartocharn with Balloch and Drymen
www.gartocharn.org

Lying on the A811 four miles east of Balloch, Gartocharn developed during the eighteenth and nineteenth centuries as demand for raw materials in Glasgow and other Scottish cities increased. Red sandstone was quarried locally and bark from oakwoods tanned the leather needed to make drive belts for cotton mills and other factories. An old jetty from where boats loaded with cargo once sailed to Balloch can still be seen on the loch shore when the water level is low.

DRYMEN

Buses connect Drymen with Balloch, Glasgow and Stirling
www.drymen.com

Drymen is a gateway to both Loch Lomond and the Trossachs, a benefit which has served it well through history. Drymen's strategic location overlooking the lowest fording point of Endrick Water has ensured plenty of passing traffic. Although the nearby Roman fort of **Drumquhassle** is little more than a cross on the map, its subtle remains show the importance of the area as far back as the first century, a time when the Romans were pushing west from Stirling in a land at the furthest reaches of their empire.

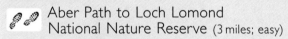

Duncryne (½ mile; easy)

Loch Lomond from Duncryne

Gartocharn means 'the place of the humped hill', which is appropriate as half a mile east lies the conical hill of **Duncryne**. A prominent feature on the southern shore of the loch, the hill boasts views northwards to Ben Lomond and the Highlands disproportionate to its height. For an easy child-friendly walk to the summit, follow the road south of the village for half a mile to a layby where a short track leaves the road and passes through woods.

Aber Path to Loch Lomond National Nature Reserve (3 miles; easy)

This path links Gartocharn with a section of **Loch Lomond National Nature Reserve** covering the mouth of Endrick Water. It is a good place to see wetland wildlife. In spring and summer osprey hunt here and wildfowl including greylag geese, wigeon and teal are among the visiting waterbirds. The waymarked path starts from the Millennium Hall, crossing fields before heading down towards the loch. After entering the nature reserve the path follows the shore to viewpoints taking in the mouth of the river and the wetlands to the south and east. Return by the same route. A walk leaflet is available from tourist information centres and Scottish Natural Heritage. For more information on Loch Lomond National Nature Reserve visit www.nnr-scotland.org.uk.

Control and conquest knocked on Drymen's door again in the eighteenth century as the government sought to tame the Highlands in the aftermath of the failed Jacobite rebellions. The subsequent programme of military road-building was designed to improve access to the region for government soldiers, aiding political control. It included a route between Stirling and Dumbarton, which passed through Drymen. However, not all traces of the clans were removed, as in 1734 Rob Roy MacGregor's sister took out a license for the Clachan Inn on the village green, which still serves customers today and is reputed to be the oldest inn in Scotland.

The road brought more than soldiers to Drymen. Increasing numbers of tourists and trade brought more visitors and prosperity to the town. Drymen developed as a livestock centre with a weekly market, a tradition continued in part today with the annual Drymen Show held at the end of May. Its accessibility meant it was also ideally placed to capitalise on Sir Walter Scott's popularisation of the area during the eighteenth century when it became a magnet for visitors to both the Trossachs and Loch Lomond. This tradition continues to the present day with the Rob Roy Way, the West Highland Way and National Cycle Route 7 all passing through the village. Cycle hire is also available (Lomond Activities ☎ 01360 660066).

To the west of Drymen is Buchanan Castle, which became the official seat of Clan Graham when it was sold by the 5th Earl of Montrose in

A prize-winning bull on display at Drymen Show

1925. For a short time afterwards it was used as a hotel and briefly saw service as a hospital during the Second World War. Its best-known patient was Rudolph Hess, Adolf Hitler's deputy in the Nazi Party, who was treated for injuries sustained while parachuting into Scotland in 1941. After the war it was de-roofed to avoid paying rates and thereafter started to deteriorate. It remains in a ruinous state today. The grounds of the castle are now a golf course.

West Highland Way

www.west-highland-way.co.uk

The West Highland Way enters the National Park at Drymen and anyone who has travelled up the eastern shore of Loch Lomond will almost certainly have encountered a West Highland Way walker. With their belongings on their back, West Highland Way walkers are a breed apart, often enduring persistent rain and penetrating midges along the 95-mile route from Milngavie, on the outskirts of Glasgow, to Fort William. Since it was opened in 1980 the 50,000 or so people who complete the walk each year have helped it to become one of the most popular long-distance paths in the UK. In many cases the money walkers spend also helps to prop up businesses and villages on the route.

The path uses ancient roads, including drovers' roads and old coaching roads and is traditionally walked from south to north. On average it takes seven or eight days to complete, although fitter and more experienced walkers do it in five or six. However fast you are, you will struggle to beat Jez Bragg who ran the entire route in under

A signpost on the West Highland Way, which runs through the National Park

16 hours on his way to winning the annual West Highland Way race in 2006.

In the National Park the route follows the eastern shore of Loch Lomond, crossing Conic Hill into Balmaha, up to Rowardennan and on to Inversnaid. From there it passes through Glen Falloch northward to Crianlarich then along Strathfillan to Tyndrum. Much of its popularity is due to the wide variety of terrains through which it passes – across lowland moors, through dense woodland and rolling hills, and over high mountainous regions – not to mention its diversity of wildlife.

Balmaha

Buses connect Balmaha with Drymen
Information centre 📞 01389 722100

Heading north from Drymen to Rowardennan, the first real sight of Loch Lomond does not come until you arrive at Balmaha. The village nestles under the shadow of **Conic Hill**, a familiar landmark for anyone walking the West Highland Way which passes through the village. This sharply rising ridge marks the line of the **Highland Boundary Fault** (see p. 11) and is an abrupt reminder that landscape does things differently in the Highlands. North of here land is not suited to growing crops and has been wooded for centuries. Balmaha marks the start of a chain of ancient oak woodlands that fringe long stretches of the loch shore and which have helped shape the livelihoods of those living here.

At first the woodlands were coppiced for charcoal to smelt iron in small bloomeries; the waste slag and charcoal from these bloomeries can still be found by keen-eyed archaeologists today. When larger, more efficient blast furnaces made the small-scale iron smelting redundant, locals turned to harvesting the oak bark for tannin, which was used to soften leather in Glasgow's tanneries and leather-finishing industries. A wood-processing plant existed in Balmaha up until 1920; its closure finally ended 250 years of working woodlands on Loch Lomond.

The link between Loch Lomond woodlands and Scotland's cities has changed from industry to leisure. Balmaha's sheltered bay makes it an ideal place for boating. Private boats now jostle for space at moorings that were once filled by barges loaded with wood products. Macfarlane's Boatyard (📞 01360 870214), a local institution for the last 150 years, offers a range of services including boat trips in two

Inchcailloch (2 miles; easy)

For a real feel of Loch Lomond's woodlands take the short boat journey from Macfarlane's Boatyard to **Inchcailloch**, one of the few easily accessible islands on Loch Lomond. Part of the Loch Lomond National Nature Reserve, the island is now protected for its wildlife, but has had a long association with human history. In the eighth century St Kentigerna, daughter of the King of Leinster, took her family from Ireland and worked as a missionary along Scotland's west coast. Eventually they arrived at Loch Lomond. By now Kentigerna was getting on in years and she settled on the island which appropriately became known as Inchcailloch – 'the island of old women'. Here she founded a nunnery where she lived until her death in AD 734. Her son became St Fillan, another notable National Park saint.

Kentigerna's spirit remained on the island and five centuries after her death a parish church was founded here. Those parishioners not living on the island dutifully rowed across the water to worship up until the seventeenth century. The burial ground was still in use up to the 1940s and many clansman from the MacFarlanes and the MacGregors are buried here.

The graveyard on Inchcailloch

The graveyard is part of a nature trail which takes you round the whole island, including the sites of ancient farms. Here inhabitants eked a subsistence living from the soil and worked the woodlands up until the end of the eighteenth century when their farms were replaced with large-scale sheep farms and the last inhabitants left the island. The path takes you to the high point on the island with views over the southern half of the loch. An enjoyable morning or afternoon can be spent exploring Inchcailloch. For the more adventurous there is a small campsite with composting toilets at the southern end of the island. Camping requires a permit which can be obtained from the National Park Authority.

For more information on Inchailloch 📞 01389 722100 or visit www.nnr-scotland.org.uk.

Conic Hill (2 miles; moderate)

Looking down the Highland Line from Conic Hill

The short walk to the summit of Conic Hill offers spectacular views over the loch and allows you to see the Highland Boundary Fault at first hand. From the car park follow the West Highland Way eastward through conifer woodlands and onto the ridge proper after about a mile. The Fault runs along the summit so you can stand with one foot in the Highlands and one foot in the Lowlands. Its path can easily be traced by joining up the line of islands in a geological dot-to-dot. Return the same way.

✦✦ Balmaha Millennium Forest Path (I mile; easy)

This easy, waymarked, low-level walk begins in the car park at Balmaha and follows woodlands to the loch shore taking in sections of the West Highland Way to the viewpoint at Craigie Fort. The path then descends and follows the loch shore southwards to Balmaha Pier. Return via the road to the car park. For full details pick up a leaflet at National Park visitor centres, or visit www. lochlomond-trossachs.org.

traditional wooden boats, a ferry service to **Inchcailloch** and a mailboat service to **Inchmurrin**, as well as fishing boat hire and the sale of fishing permits. The village is the last stop on the eastern shore for buses and there is a large car park, which soon fills up on summer days. There is also a National Park Visitor Centre which has displays and information about the area.

THE ROAD TO ROWARDENNAN

There are no more settlements north of Balmaha. One mile or so north of the village there is a shoreside picnic area run by the National Park Authority at **Milarrochy Bay**, where you can also launch and register boats. Carry on another mile and you reach **Cashel Forest**, an ambitious native woodland project begun in 1996 by the Royal Scottish Forestry Society to create a new, working, native woodland on the shores of Loch

Ben Lomond Memorial Park

Lomond at Cashel Farm. Visitors can see how the project is progressing and enjoy a choice of walks around the site. There is parking and a small visitor centre on the site. Waymarked walks range from 1 to 4 miles (www.cashel.org.uk or phone 01360 870450 for more information).

Just beyond Cashel is the start of the **Ben Lomond Memorial Park**. Opened in 1997, the park was created out of the former Rowardennan estate with the support of the National Heritage Memorial Fund. Most of the land is owned by the Forestry Commission Scotland and the National Trust for Scotland. The area is permanently protected as a memorial to those Scots who made the ultimate sacrifice during the Second World War. There are more woodland walks starting from the Forestry Commission Scotland's shoreside picnic site 1 mile further north at **Sallochy Bay**. Three waymarked routes range in length from 1 to 5 miles.

ROWARDENNAN

Rowardennan marks the end of the line along the eastern shore of the loch unless you are following the West Highland Way on foot through the wooded lochside. Beyond the hotel, the road ends at a parking and picnic area adjacent to an unmanned information centre with toilets. A track leads from here to the youth hostel. The best way to get to Rowardennan by public transport is on the ferry from Inverbeg on the western shore, otherwise it is an 8-mile walk up the road from Balmaha.

INVERSNAID

A post bus operates between Aberfoyle post office and Inversnaid Monday–Saturday departing at 10 a.m. and returning at 2.40 p.m.

Although there is a small community at Inversnaid, its main focus is the lochside hotel. To our car-focused society Inversnaid may seem a strange place to build a hotel. Bounded by Loch Lomond on one side

The falls at Inversnaid

and a tortuous 16-mile road to Aberfoyle on the other, it is not a place easily reached. However, Inversnaid is a product of the Victorian era and in the past would have seemed anything but remote. Even Queen Victoria herself paid a visit while touring Scotland in 1869.

The Victorian thirst for travel flowed naturally into the country Sir Walter Scott had immortalised in his writings and during the latter half of the nineteenth century the Trossachs Tour was born. This was a day trip from Glasgow or Edinburgh involving trains, boats and horse-drawn coaches. Trains took travellers to Balloch, where steamers plied the loch to Inversnaid. Coaches then covered the short journey to Stronachlachar on Loch Katrine, from where the steamer to Trossachs Pier brought travellers into the heart of Scott's *The Lady of the Lake* country. The return journey was by coach, most commonly to Callander, where trains ran to Edinburgh and Glasgow. The more ambitious made journeys northwards to Crianlarich and Oban, bypassing Inversnaid and continuing to Ardlui instead. The hotel became an essential stopping point and the volume of travellers ensured a healthy trade. Today most visitors arrive by car from Aberfoyle, although Cruise Loch Lomond and the Inversnaid Hotel operate boat services to Inveruglas and Tarbet.

Ben Lomond (6 miles; difficult)

www.nts.org.uk

Most people visit Rowardennan either as part of the West Highland Way or to make the pilgrimage up **Ben Lomond**, Scotland's most southerly Munro and a national treasure. A Scottish Natural Heritage survey found Ben Lomond to be the most popular Munro in Scotland, with 10 per cent of the adult population having climbed it and over 30,000 people heading for its summit every year. No doubt this is due in part to its accessibility from Scotland's Central Belt; it is possible to leave Glasgow, climb Ben Lomond in the afternoon and be back for supper. Its popularity also makes maintenance of the path a problem for the National Trust for Scotland which owns the mountain and spends a good deal of time and money each year repairing its paths.

The paternal peak casts its spell over the loch and has bewitched visitors for centuries, leading early climbers into wild bouts of over-exaggeration. When John Stoddart climbed the mountain in 1799 he wrote, 'That which you look toward as an unbroken surface, upon your approach becomes divided by impassable valleys: an unheard rill becomes a roaring torrent, and a gentle slope is found to be an unscalable cliff'.

Ben Lomond, Scotland's most southerly Munro

The truth is somewhat less fanciful. The 6-mile route begins on the waymarked path leading from the information centre through forest before emerging on the lower slopes of Sron Aonaich. It is an easy walk along this broad south-facing ridge. The final slope steepens to reach the rim of the mountain's north-east corrie that is then followed to the top. While Stoddart's description of the ascent may be questionable, many who have stood here on a clear day, with much of the National Park spread out below, would share his emotion when he writes, 'It seemed as if I had been suddenly transported into a new state of existence, cut off from every meaner association and invisibly united with the surrounding purity and brightness'.

For variety, return via the north-west ridge taking in the summit of Ptarmigan and descend its south ridge to hit the lochside road about half a mile north of the Rowardennan car park. Although it is the views which draw most people to the mountain, its ecology is important too. Ben Lomond offers a natural progression from the loch shore through woodlands, to heathlands and finally high-altitude alpine habitats. Such transitions are rare in this part of Scotland and the mountain has a variety of wildlife, including a handful of ptarmigan, adders, feral goats and rare alpine flowers.

A Night Ascent of Ben Lomond

From the Scottish Mountaineering Club Journal, *Volume 3, Number 4, January 1895*

On 13th September, Messrs Lyon, M'Millan, Coubrough (non-members), and I took the evening train from Glasgow to Balloch, and starting thence about 10 p.m. walked up the shores of Loch Lomond to Rowardennan, and climbed the Ben in time to see the sun rise. My fancy still lingers fondly round that moonlight walk; there was an inexpressible charm about it. The night was simply perfect, the moon full, hardly a breath of wind stirred the still waters of the loch, and all around slept the silence of the hills. It was one of those scenes of perfect beauty that are happily not unfamiliar to the lover of the mountains, and that remain as pictures in the mind for a lifetime.

The moon had set before we reached Rowardennan, and during the first part of the ascent there was a good deal of groping after the path. But when we struck the crest of the long southern shoulder of the hill, there were the first streaks of early dawn already lighting up the eastern hills with a feeble glimmer, which steadily grew brighter and stronger, until, while we were still a short way from the summit, the sun itself shot up in a blaze of glory from a bank of cloud. Breakfast was enjoyed at the spring near the top, under its benign influence, but at that hour Boreas was stronger than Sol.

The whole northern view, but especially the line of hills from Ben More and Stobinian to Ben Cruachan, was remarkably fine. The early morning clouds capped many a familiar summit, or veiled many a rugged mountain shape in their fleecy folds, leaving the dark peaks floating above them, inky black in contrast to their whiteness. All around, on every hill, seemed to be the home of cloudland, but Ben Lomond itself was visited by only one or two stray wisps and wreaths of mist. It was not till we were sailing down to Balloch that the heavy masses settled down. In the east, the most interesting objects were Stirling Castle and the Wallace Monument, both standing like islands in a golden haze.

A pleasant scamper brought us down to Rowardennan just in time to catch the first steamer to Balloch; and a delightful expedition was brought to a close by a charming sail homewards on the broad-bosomed loch.

 ## Ardess History Trail (2 miles; easy)

National Trust for Scotland Ranger Service 01360 870224

While many may see Rowardennan as being remote, it has long been a place of people. Rob Roy owned land in the Ardess area between 1711 and 1713 and there are many other traces of the people who have lived here over the centuries. For a less strenuous excursion than the ascent of Ben Lomond, the **Ardess History Trail** offers an opportunity to explore some of this history. This 2-mile trail uncovers house sites, ancient agriculture, iron ore smelting sites and even evidence of illicit whisky stills: an archaeological journey of the last 300 years. The circular trail starts at the National Trust for Scotland ranger centre at Ardess. To get there follow the West Highland Way north from the Rowardennan car park. Pick up a trail leaflet at the ranger base and walk to the trailhead.

 ## West Highland Way Taster (9 miles; moderate)

Buses and trains call at Tarbet
Cruise Loch Lomond 01301 702356; **www.cruiselochlomond.co.uk**

There is a way to enjoy the beauty of the Loch Lomond woodlands without needing the endurance of a West Highland Way walker. Cruise Loch Lomond operates boats which run daily at 10 a.m. from Tarbet Pier between Easter and October. Forty-five minutes later you arrive at Rowardennan, from where you can then follow the West Highland Way north for 9 miles to Inversnaid through Craigroyston Woods. These special Atlantic oak woods are a product of Loch Lomond's mild, wet climate. They are a haven for moisture-loving mosses, lichens and ferns, and are protected for their wildlife. You may even catch sight of some of Loch Lomond's

famous feral goats. This path takes you through Rob Roy country and there are many legends about his life in these parts. Be sure to arrive at Inversnaid in good time as the only way back to Tarbet is to catch the Cruise Loch Lomond boat at 4.30 p.m. from Inversnaid Pier.

 Inversnaid Nature Reserve (various)

www.rspb.org.uk

Ironically, for a building originally constructed for military purposes, Garrison Farm was acquired by the RSPB in 2002 and is now part of the **Inversnaid Nature Reserve**. The RSPB is taking forward its ambitious plans to expand the area of native woodland through regeneration and careful planting.

There are three trails on the reserve: along the West Highland Way, following the eastern shore of Loch Lomond through the reserve starting from Inversnaid; a woodland trail which detours off the West Highland Way about 500 metres north of the Inversnaid car park; and the Garrison track which is about 800 metres long and leads to a renovated sheep enclosure which is a great place to view moorland wildlife. This third track starts from Garrison Farm car park.

Park People – Rob Roy MacGregor

Rob Roy's Grave, Balquhidder

Arguably the most colourful character associated with the National Park area, Rob Roy MacGregor was born in Glengyle, at the head of Loch Katrine in 1671. He made the territory between Loch Lomond and Balquhidder his hunting ground and earned a reputation as an expert, albeit slightly maverick, cattle dealer. He ran a type of protection racket common enough in that business, at that time and place: for a price he would guarantee the safety of the cattle belonging to his 'clients'. He was at least as good as his word, and he gained a reputation for his skill in tracking down and retrieving cattle stolen by others.

So good was Rob Roy's business that by 1700 he owned 7,000 acres to the north-east of Loch Lomond. In 1712 his landlord, the influential Duke of Montrose, advanced him the then colossal sum of £1,000. Unfortunately his head drover who had been dispatched with the money to buy cattle further north never returned, leaving Rob Roy himself to face the music when he defaulted on the loan. He failed to attend a court summons and was officially declared an outlaw. Montrose sent troops to our red-haired hero's Loch Lomondside home at Craigroystan, south of Inversnaid, where his wife and children were evicted and the house set alight.

Naturally unhappy with his treatment, Rob Roy's response was to exact revenge on Montrose by gathering a band of followers and raiding the duke's tenants for cattle, grain and on occasion rent, so beginning the audacious banditry that would make him famous. Things reached a head when Rob Roy and his men kidnapped John Graham of Killearn, Montrose's factor, while he was collecting rent from tenants, and imprisoned him on a small island on Loch Katrine. A ransom was sought for his return, although he later allowed the factor to go unharmed when no money was forthcoming.

This was the last straw for Montrose who persuaded the commander of government troops in Scotland to build a barracks at Inversnaid in the heart of MacGregor territory. Construction began in 1718 and the first troops were posted in 1720. Its impact was not immediate, as one of Rob Roy's first tasks once the barracks were completed was to trick his way in and set them alight. Occupation of the garrison was short-lived; the pacification of the Highlands picked up pace thereafter and the last occupants left in the 1790s, after which the site became a farm, as it still is today.

The political shift seems to have had an affect on Rob Roy. He gradually began to move his base further from Inversnaid, to the head of Balquhidder Glen, where for the most part he stayed out of the headlines. There are many tales of his exploits and miraculous escapes, some true and some the stuff of legend. Perhaps the most remarkable feat for a man who spent so much of his life fighting for one cause or another is that he died peacefully in his bed in 1734. His grave lies in Balquhidder and is a popular place of pilgrimage.

Places to visit associated with Rob Roy MacGregor:

Glengyle – Loch Katrine. Rob Roy's birthplace.

Rob Roy's Cave – A short walk from Inversnaid Hotel into Craigroyston Woods leads to the cave from where he is reputed to have planned his raids.

Inversnaid Garrison – The remains of the garrison have been incorporated into Garrison Farm adjacent to the Inversnaid Nature Reserve.

Inverlochlarig, Balquhidder – This is where Rob Roy died. Now a working farm producing venison and lamb (www.inverlochlarig.com). There is a picnic area and car park from where ascents of the glen's Munros can be made.

Balquhidder Church – The site of Rob Roy's grave.

The Western Shore

Much of the western shore of Loch Lomond is dominated by the A82, a major transport artery linking Glasgow with western Scotland. Good travel links are vital in rural areas, but the inevitable downside is that having such a major road in close proximity to the loch can spoil the visitor's experience. Having said that, there is still much to be explored and the western shore has the advantage of being well served by public transport, with regular bus services as well as access to the West Highland Railway.

WEST LOCH LOMOND CYCLE PATH

One benefit of upgrading a road is that you can turn the old road into a cycle path and this is what has happened with the West Loch Lomond Cycle Path, a 15-mile cycleway and footpath between Balloch and Tarbet. The path is traffic-free for most of the way, with only three short sections on minor roads. It is suitable for cyclists, walkers, wheelchair users and horse-riders. The route begins and ends near railway stations so you can return by train and it passes through Luss where refreshments are available. A leaflet on the cycleway is available from tourist information centres.

A colourful boat moored on Loch Lomondside

Luss

Buses connect Luss with Balloch, Glasgow, Crianlarich, Inveraray, Oban and Fort William

Information centre 📞 01389 722120

Luss is a popular stopping point with travellers and coach parties. Its large car park is crowded in summer and the lochside picnic site is popular with families. The streets of this picturesque conservation village are largely traffic-free, adding to its appeal, and there is a long sandy beach ideal for picnics and paddling. Despite being known in Gaelic as Clachan Dubh – 'the dark village' – Luss has a long Christian history dating back to the arrival of St Kessog from Munster in Ireland in the sixth century. The first recorded laird of the House of Luss claimed to be hereditary guardian of St Kessog's pastoral staff. When the sixth laird died in 1385, his daughter succeeded him and her marriage to local clan chieftain Robert de Colquhoun united the two families. Luss has remained Colquhoun territory ever since.

Luss still bears the legacy of the Colquhoun clan. By the eighteenth century, like many other places around the loch, local industry was centred on supplying raw materials to Scotland's expanding cities. There were several mills nearby including a corn mill, a sawmill and a cotton mill as well as a slate quarry. It was during this time, around 1850, that the laird cleared the old turf-thatched cottages and built a new model village for his workers, which can still be seen in the characteristic cottages lining the village streets today.

 Walks from Luss (various)

The National Park Authority has produced a leaflet detailing four short walks around Luss. For more information ask at the National Park Visitor Centre. More ambitious walkers could try an ascent of Beinn Dubh to the east of Luss. Take the path across the A82 heading up Glen Luss. A trail leads north from the road up the shoulder of Beinn Dubh and offers fine views of Ben Lomond. To descend, continue round the horseshoe-shaped trail to the Glen Luss road and follow this back to Luss.

Park People – St Kessog

Luss Church

A prince of Cashel in Ireland, St Kessog came to Scotland in AD 510 and settled on Inchtavannach – the island of the monk's house – opposite Luss. While in Ireland he was said to have miraculously revived some boys after a drowning accident and in Scotland he spent his time as a missionary bishop in south Perthshire and the Loch Lomond area. Some claim that Kessog was in effect patron saint of Scotland before Andrew, and that at Bannockburn Robert the Bruce urged on his troops in the name of 'blessed Kessog'. Several churches in Scotland are dedicated to him including ones at Luss (in Callander St Kessog's Church is now the visitor information centre) and there are records of an ancient fair being held on the feast of St Kessog at Comrie, Callander and Auchterarder.

St Kessog is said to have been martyred on 10 March 560, a mile and a half south of Luss at Bandry, where a cairn to his name become a focus of pilgrimage until the Reformation and was later demolished by road builders during the eighteenth century. In Luss Church are displayed three artifacts removed from the cairn when it was demolished to make way for the road: a carved stone head thought to represent the saint; an ancient stone font; and a stone effigy of a bishop which some believe to be Kessog himself. The present church at Luss was built in 1875, but recent archeological excavations in preparation for a new golf club nearby substantiate claims of there being a site of worship here for nearly 1,500 years.

Places to visit associated with St Kessog:

Luss Parish Church – The church has a pilgrimage centre with historic information.

Inchtavannach – St Kessog founded a monastery here in the 6th century. The island is privately owned, but can be viewed from the lochside road.

Callander – St Kessog was said to have preached from the Tom na Chesaig – 'the Hill of Kessog' beside the river Teith off Bridge Street.

The Colquhouns were involved in one of the bloodiest battles to take place on Loch Lomond's shores, in 1603. Two young MacGregors were heading home to their land at Inversnaid, and having been benighted on the western shore sought shelter from the Colquhouns, near Luss, but were refused. At this breach of hospitality they found a hut and killed a sheep for food. Unfortunately this contravened clan law and the next day they were arrested and sentenced to hang, which they did. This provocation led to what later became known as the Battle of Glen Fruin where MacGregors met Colquhouns and a vicious fight ensued.

The facts of the battle depend on which clan history you read, but it seems that despite being outnumbered the MacGregors fought on. The main contingent of the MacGregor forces attacked their enemies head on, with a smaller force flanking the Colquhouns. The Colquhouns' advantage of having a large number of cavalry was turned into a disadvantage by the boggy ground of the glen, and the MacGregors pressed on to rout the Colquhouns and their allies. A memorial to the battle stands just outside the National Park boundary, 2 miles east of Garelochhead.

They may have defeated the Colquhouns but the MacGregors paid a heavy price. An angry King James VI gave his order to 'extirpate Clan Gregor and to ruit oot their posteritie and name'. The use of the names Gregor or MacGregor was proscribed, and those who had borne the name were forbidden to carry arms. For more than 150 years the MacGregors were hunted down by their enemies. Warrants for their extermination were put on public sale as though they were to be killed

Boarding the Inchcailloch ferry

for sport. Their women were branded on the cheek, their homes burned, their livestock and possessions carried off, their families left destitute. It is not without meaning, then, that the clan motto, inscribed on Rob Roy MacGregor's grave, is 'MacGregor Despite Them'.

There is more about local clan history at the **Clan Colquhoun Visitor Centre & Luss Museum**, in Hall House on the main street (✆ 01389 850564).

LOCH LOMOND'S ISLANDS

www.lochlomondtrossachs.org.uk

No one really knows how many islands there are on Loch Lomond. Some are there one day and submerged the next. Many have fascinating histories, greatly illuminated by a study carried out in the late 1990s by the Friends of Loch Lomond, which recorded over 390 new archaeological sites. Unfortunately, as interesting as they are, getting to the islands is problematic. Only three islands are in public ownership: Inchcailloch, Bucinch and Ceardach, the former being owned by Scottish Natural Heritage and the latter two by the National Trust for Scotland. Access to these islands is free, but in the interests of wildlife no dogs should be taken onto the islands. Macfarlane's Boatyard in Balmaha runs ferries to Inchcailloch and operates a mailboat to Inchmurrin (see Introduction and Balmaha sections for details). On Inchmurrin there is a hotel which also operates a ferry service for customers departing from a jetty close to the Arden roundabout on the A82 (see p. 17).

Although mostly uninhabited today, the islands have a long history of occupation. Security and ease of access made them attractive places to be and all of the islands have evidence of human habitation from prehistoric times. Earliest settlers often chose to live on crannogs, artificial islands attached either to other islands or the shore by a bridge or a causeway across which inhabitants could retreat overnight. There are at least ten crannogs in Loch Lomond. However, since they were ordinarily built of wood, few signs remain and tracking them down is not easy. The Kitchen, a small island visible from the south shore of Inchcailloch, is the easiest crannog for visitors to see.

Other island dwellers left more obvious evidence of their presence as local clan leaders built castles on a handful of islands, the remains of which are still here today. War and pestilence persuaded the Earls of Lennox to retreat to Inchmurrin during the fourteenth century. The MacFarlanes built a castle on Ellan Vhow in the north of the loch. A spectacular keep on Inchgalbraith, which covers more than half of the island, was built by the Clan Galbraith during the fifteenth century. Sadly, there is no defence against time and many of these ruins are in danger of being lost forever.

The discovery of a large complex of illicit stills on Inchfad was evidence that the illegal whisky trade was alive and well in Loch Lomond in the past. Private distilling was banned in 1781, but that failed to prevent a huge trade in smuggled whisky from the Highlands and islands like Inchfad. Business improved during the Napoleonic War period when imported alcohol was in short supply.

Although excise men were employed to track down whisky smugglers, landowners often turned a blind eye as the trade brought income for their tenants. Operations were well organised on Inchfad. The essential ingredients were all within easy reach: grain would have been shipped up the river Leven, peat probably came from nearby Inchmoan, and there would have been plenty of wood available locally.

THE ROAD TO CRIANLARICH

The road north of Luss hugs the loch shoreline, offering occasional glimpses of the water. After 3 miles you come to **Inverbeg**, where a ferry leaves for Rowardennan. Two miles further on is **Firkin Point**, a seasonal picnic area with car parking and toilets as well as a stretch of shingle beach. The lochside path here stretches north and south for a couple of miles in either direction and is ideal for wheelchair users, families with prams and those who want to get close to the loch. Three

Ben Lomond from Dubh Lochan

miles further on you arrive at **Tarbet** where the road splits, west to Loch Long and Argyll and east to Crianlarich. **Cruise Loch Lomond** boats leave from the pier here and there are hotels, toilets, a post office and a visitor information centre. It is also a stopping-off point for the West Highland Railway. There are a couple of short forest walks from the village.

Beyond Tarbet Loch Lomond narrows and deepens, becoming more fjord-like. At **Inveruglas** there is parking, toilets and a picnic area and this is also where the seasonal ferry crosses over to the Inversnaid Hotel. Stretching up the slopes of Ben Vorlich like fingers are the pipelines of the **Loch Sloy hydro-electricity station**. Built in 1950, this scheme is the largest conventional hydro scheme in the UK. A 2-mile tunnel carries water from Loch Sloy, under Ben Vorlich, and down the mountain via four pipelines to the power station. It is capable of generating 150 megawatts and can go from standing still to full load in around 5 minutes. Hydro-electricity has been a controversial subject in Loch Lomond. In 1978 plans for a power station on Ben Lomond so outraged local resident Hannah Stirling that she wrote a letter to the *Glasgow Herald* asking for volunteers to support her in fighting the scheme. People responded in their hundreds and the Friends of Loch Lomond were born. The plans were scrapped and the Friends of Loch Lomond & The Trossachs as they are now known have carried on their work protecting the area for three decades.

The next stop on the West Highland Railway is **Ardlui**, at the northernmost tip of Loch Lomond. Ardlui's popularity grew from its location as a connecting point between steamers from Inversnaid and road transport further north during Victorian times. In summer the Ardlui Hotel runs a ferry to Ardleish (☏ 01301 704243) which is regularly used by West Highland Way walkers and gives access to the northernmost stretches of the Loch Lomond woodlands. A short walk north of Ardleish brings you to Cnap Mor, a low hill that offers arguably the best view of the loch. Nearby Gael Loch and Dubh Lochan are also important sites for nature conservation.

As you travel north of Ardlui, Loch Lomond is left behind. It feels strange not to be sharing this part of the journey with the loch's expanse of water. The landscape between Ardlui and Crianlarich is more open, with fewer distinguishing features accompanying the river Falloch as it tumbles down the glen. A car park and picnic site mark the **Falls of Falloch**, where the river cascades over a band of stubborn rock. Up on the slopes north of the falls is an ancient boundary stone known as the Clach nam Breatann – 'the **Stone of the Britons**', which is said to mark the defeat of the Britons of Strathclyde by the Scotii of Dalriada in AD 717, and may well have acted as a boundary stone between the two cultures and the Picts who lived to the north-east. Six hundred years later Robert the Bruce passed by the same way on his return from fighting the English at the Battle of Methven.

Easy to miss in the rush to reach Crianlarich are the **Glen Falloch pinewoods**. Another sign of arrival in the Highlands, this small area of Scots pine forest covering knolls to the east of the road is the most southerly remnant of the ancient Caledonian pinewood which once covered a large part of the Scottish Highlands. You can get a closer look by stopping in the lay-by a mile south of Crianlarich and following the track under the railway before turning south and crossing the deer fencing, but the terrain is difficult and there is no path. Soon after, the road and rail descend into Crianlarich and the high country of Breadalbane.

Opposite: Inchmahome Priory

PART THREE

THE TROSSACHS

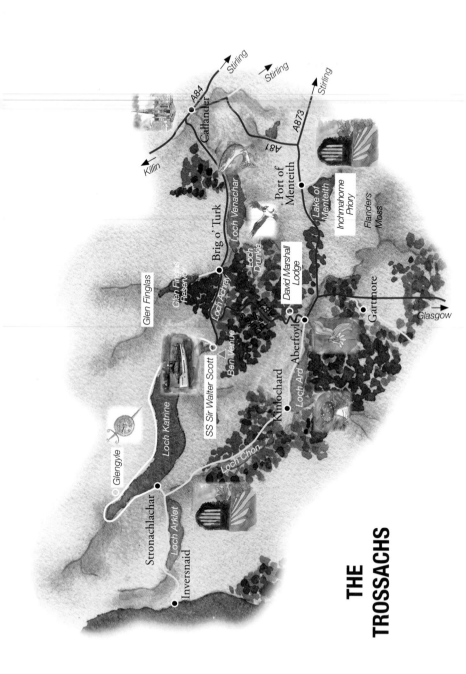

THE
TROSSACHS

The Trossachs

Panorama of the Trossachs

'Where are the Trossachs?' sounds like a good question for a pub quiz. Purists will tell you that, strictly speaking, the name applies to the short, rocky, wooded pass approaching Loch Katrine from Loch Achray. However, it is better known as a description of a wider area of the surrounding countryside: a triangular wedge of the National Park north-east of Loch Lomond, whose boundaries are slightly blurred, but include Aberfoyle, Callander, Lake of Menteith, Loch Katrine and Loch Ard. What the area's name means is harder still to pin down and even the most fastidious etymologist may end up disappointed by an unsatisfactory conclusion. What is undisputed is the beauty of this landscape, often subtitled 'Scotland in miniature', reflecting the flavour of wider Highland scenery that can be tasted here, but in a compact accessible form.

Some may argue that it is the Trossachs and not Loch Lomond that is the jewel in the National Park's crown. This rivalry is reflected in each being designated a National Scenic Area and explains the equal weight given to the two areas in the National Park's name. However, the Trossachs does have a unique claim to fame as the place where Romantic tourism began in Scotland. The area around Loch Katrine will be associated with Sir Walter Scott long after the last sailing of the steamship which bears his name.

While cultural associations abound in the Trossachs, its landscape is more than simply the setting for a good book. The area is famed for its woodlands, which in spring are covered in bluebells and in autumn are lush with mushrooms. This is the forest heart of the National Park. Here it is possible to watch osprey fishing, red kites flying, deer running and red squirrels jumping. The David Marshall Lodge north of Aberfoyle offers an ideal base for exploring the natural beauty and wildlife of the area, all around and just waiting to be discovered.

Mushrooms are the autumn harvest in the Trossachs

Less tangible is the supernatural side of the Trossachs. Fairies, goblins and wee folk are all threaded into the fabric of the region's story, from one legend behind the naming of Loch Katrine to another set in the graveyards of Aberfoyle.

The Trossachs offers a huge variety of activities: you can climb the crags of Ben A'an, sail the waters of Loch Venachar, cycle the shores of Loch Katrine, follow the footsteps of Rob Roy, ride the route of Queen Victoria, picnic on the bank of river Teith or go elf hunting on Fairy Hill. The Trossachs is a destination in itself.

Gartmore

Buses connect Gartmore to Glasgow via Balfron and Stirling

Although now mostly bypassed by visitors hastening between Glasgow and Aberfoyle on the A81, Gartmore has not always been as overlooked. The village lies on an eighteenth-century drover's road along which cattle were driven from Skye and the west Highlands to markets in Falkirk. The name Gartmore means 'the big field or enclosure' and here cattle would be rested and traded. Rob Roy MacGregor was among those who bought cattle at Gartmore fairs.

The current village dates back to the eighteenth century when Nicol Graham, the local laird, set about developing what was to be one of the first planned estate villages in Scotland. He wanted a community to help grow his estate and brought in a brewer, a shoemaker, a tailor, a surgeon, several merchants and a minister. The Black Bull pub dates back to 1700 and the school and the church are both eighteenth-century buildings.

Gartmore, the birthplace of Robert Cunninghame Graham

Graham also built Gartmore House, a fine mansion which shelters behind woodlands on the far side of the playing fields. It is now a private hotel, but in 1852 it was the birthplace of one of Scotland's most flamboyant heroes, **Robert Bontine Cunninghame Graham**. Financial circumstances forced his family to rent out Gartmore House, so with nowhere to call home, he set off to Argentina before he was 20 to become a gaucho, dealing in horses and cattle.

Don Roberto, as he became affectionately known, went on to be a writer, world traveller, champion of the poor, and political leader, as well as retaining an interest in Gartmore as the local laird. He was MP for north-west Lanarkshire and in the 1920s became the first president of the National Party of Scotland, which became the Scottish National Party. His enduring passion, however, was for horses. When he died in Argentina in 1936, his hearse was pulled through the streets of Buenos

Aires by his two favourite mounts wearing black plumes. He is buried alongside his wife in the family burial ground on Inchmahome. A monument, owned by the National Trust for Scotland, commemorating his life and his horses stands across the playing fields on the north side of the village (for more information visit www.nts.org.uk).

National Cycle Route 7 and the Rob Roy Way pass through the village. Cycle hire is available locally (☎ 01877 382614; www.trossachscycles.co.uk). Gartmore lies close to the centre of the Queen Elizabeth Forest Park and offers plenty of opportunities to enjoy the surrounding areas.

ROB ROY WAY

Rob Roy Way: **www.robroyway.com**
Rob Roy Challenge: **www.robroychallenge.com**

Starting from Drymen, this unoffical long-distance route follows a mixture of paths, tracks and quiet roads to the Perthshire town of Pitlochry. From Drymen it winds its way north-eastwards, often accompanying National Cycle Route 7, through Aberfoyle, Callander, Lochearnhead and on to Killin, where it leaves the National Park.

There are remote moorland sections where wildlife abounds and panoramic views over Ben Vorlich, the Trossachs and Ben Lawers, crossing country Rob Roy would have known well. The Way provides some choice about the route at various points, allowing the walker to determine the length of the overall walk, and the countryside and

In spring Aberfoyle's woodlands are carpeted in bluebells

villages visited. Depending on route choice, the distance is between 79 miles and 92.5 miles.

The more energetic may want to have a go at the **Rob Roy Challenge**. This charity event covers up to 55 miles of the Rob Roy Way, from Drymen to Kenmore, by a combination of walking and cycling. Various options on the challenge also allow competitors to opt for shorter routes ending at Balquhidder or Killin.

ABERFOYLE

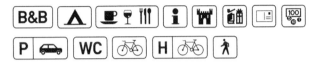

Buses connect Aberfoyle with Glasgow, via Balfron and Stirling
Information centre 📞 08707 200604; **www.aberfoyle.co.uk**

The impact of the Highland Boundary Fault on the landscape of the Loch Lomond & The Trossachs National Park is clearly conspicuous on the southern approach to Aberfoyle. The undulating line of the A81 scores the low-lying, flood-prone mosses covering the land to the south of the Fault. Ahead the Highlands rise like a wall, the Menteith Hills are to the east, and Craigmore and Ben Venue are to the west. The distinction could hardly be clearer cut. Aberfoyle is cradled beneath the hills on a crossroads astride the Fault.

As well as shaping the area's geography, the Fault has helped to define its character. Aberfoyle's most famous inhabitant was the seventeenth-century clergyman **Rev. Robert Kirk**, who, at the wave of a wand, was transformed from being a respectable man of the cloth to announcing that he could communicate with fairies. His story has become synonymous with the village. More fantastic interpretations put Aberfoyle's enchanted reputation down to its location over the Fault, asserting that the associated electromagnetic forces make supernatural happenings more likely.

Whatever the truth behind Rev. Kirk's fairy tale, his tombstone can be found in the graveyard of the old church to the south of the village centre, across the ancient humpback bridge over the infant river Forth. As well as Kirk's grave there are several cast-iron, coffin-shaped mort safes. These beefed-up burial plots are thought to have been needed as protection from body snatchers, whether criminal or supernatural, who might want to spirit away the recently deceased. From the graveyard the road continues south past the Old Manse, once frequented by Sir Walter Scott on writing trips to the Trossachs. Beyond the Old Manse,

Park People – Rev. Robert Kirk

Fairy

Few people associated with the National Park can be said to have lived a life of such contrast as Robert Kirk. He was born in Aberfoyle in 1640 in the Old Manse across the river from today's bustling village centre. As the seventh son of the parish minister, Kirk followed his father into the cloth and became minister at Balquhidder in 1669. Here he distinguished himself not only in his pastoral duties over a territory which stretched as far as Loch Lomond, but also in his theological research. He translated 100 psalms into Gaelic and re-wrote Bedell's Gaelic Bible in Roman characters as Scots could not read the original Irish letters. Copies were distributed to every parish in the Highlands.

If all you read of Rev. Kirk came from his two decades ministering at Balquhidder, then you would not believe it was the same Rev. Kirk who returned to Aberfoyle when the parish became vacant in 1685. Behind the Old Manse, where young Robert Kirk had played as a boy, was the domed summit of Doon Hill, which, translated from the

Gaelic, means 'Fairy Hill'. Soon after his return to the parish, Kirk began venturing onto the hill, often at the dead of night, where, now convinced of the existence of the wee folk, he would spend many nights talking with them, believing that they had chosen him to interpret their thoughts to the outside world.

In 1690 he collated the findings of his fairy wanderings into a book: *The Secret Commonwealth of Elves, Fauns and Fairies.* This was a far cry from his previous works and brought with it considerable risk as such a publication would almost certainly have been interpreted as witchcraft. This was punishable at the time by strangulation at the stake and burning to death.

Kirk didn't have to worry about such a fate as two years later he was found dead in his nightshirt on Doon Hill, some say spirited away by the wee folk. However he died, what was true was that this was not his last appearance. Following his funeral he visited his cousin with a simple request. He was not dead he claimed, but had been carried away by the fairies to their world beneath Doon Hill. He would reappear at his son's forthcoming baptism where he would come back to life if his relative, Graham of Duchray, threw a knife at his head, for fairies feared iron and the knife would force them to release him.

True to his word, Kirk showed up as large as life at the baptism in the Old Manse. Although Graham of Duchray had brought a knife with him, so paralysed with fear was he that he could not throw it. Kirk's figure left the room and was never seen again. The truth behind the events of that time has been a source of controversy ever since. However, to wander among the graves of the old churchyard and look upon Kirk's sandstone tomb, which some say has always been bereft of a body, can still bring shivers down your spine.

Places to visit associated with Rev. Robert Kirk:

Balquhidder Church – Kirk was minisiter here for two decades from 1669.

Kirkton of Aberfoyle Cemetery – Burial place of Rev. Kirk.

Doon Hill – Site of Kirk's supernatural encounters.

a Forestry Commission for Scotland walk takes you onto Doon Hill and the scene of Rev. Kirk's encounters with the wee folk.

Before 1800 Aberfoyle was just a small hamlet centred around the old church. It was the coming of the railway in 1884 which changed all that. Trains were needed to transport slate from the quarry up on the Duke's Pass (see below) to Glasgow to feed the insatiable demand for roofing for the city's expanding population. Although the quarries have been silent for half a century, they were worked for more than 300 years and in 1858–9 produced 1.4 million slates. After the arrival of the railway, activity in Aberfoyle moved north of the river and even today its impact can be seen despite the railway being closed for half a century. The car park is sited where the station used to be and the old line can be walked or cycled as far south as Buchlyvie.

The railway not only took raw materials out, but it brought tourists in. Sir Walter Scott had set the flame of Romanticism ablaze and the Victorians came in their droves to experience it. In Aberfoyle their unbridled enthusiasm turned fiction into fact. In his novel *Rob Roy*, one of Scott's characters, Baillie Nicol Jarvie, gets into a fight at an inn in the village. Finding himself swordless he defends himself with a red-hot poker taken from the fire.

Undeterred by the absence of fact, travellers flocked to see where the fight had taken place. Obligingly, the Baillie Nicol Jarvie Hotel soon sprang up and the poker which it was claimed Jarvie had used was hung from an oak in the village. The hotel has now been converted into apartments, but the Poker Oak (complete with poker) still stands in the village.

More information on the history of Aberfoyle can be found at the **Trossachs Discovery Centre** in the centre of the village. The other main attraction in the village is the **Scottish Wool Centre** (📞 01877 382850) adjacent to the main car park, which houses outlets for major wool retailers, hosts displays and shows, and has a restaurant.

QUEEN ELIZABETH FOREST PARK

David Marshall Lodge 📞 01877 382258; **www.forestry.gov.uk/scotland**

Aberfoyle lies at the centre of the Queen Elizabeth Forest Park, created by the Forestry Commission in 1953 to celebrate the inauguration of the eponymous monarch. Stretching from the east shore of Loch Lomond almost to Callander, the Forest Park is the largest forest in Great Britain and almost three-quarters of the area is covered with trees. While timber production is a key industry, it also offers plenty of choice for recreation, whether on foot, cycle, horseback or even a husky sled. Visitors can travel for miles through the Forest Park on the network of maintained paths. There are a dozen or so car parks, and bus links to trailheads.

The best place to get a flavour for the Forest Park is the **David Marshall Lodge**, half a mile north of Aberfoyle at the top of a series of steep hairpin bends. The climb is rewarded by glorious views across the southern half of the forest and towards Ben Lomond. In summer you can watch footage of local ospreys relayed live to the centre. There is a restaurant, shops and exhibitions about the forest. A Go Ape high-wire adventure course offers on-site excitement. The centre is an ideal stopping point for lunch or a picnic and a wide range of walks leave from the lodge.

Just west of Aberfoyle, a trailhead at the eastern end of Loch Ard offers routes for walkers and cyclists, including the **Loch Ard Sculpture Trail**, a network of family-friendly paths with art installations en route. North of David Marshall Lodge the road passes the disused Aberfoyle Quarries and drops down into the heart of the Trossachs. This is the **Duke's Pass**, a stunning high-level route along which you could imagine its architect, the Duke of Montrose, riding his horse, over the twisting climb to reach his hunting lodge on the shore of Loch Achray, on the site of the current Loch Achray Hotel. For an intimate taste of the

Looking into the heart of the Trossachs from the Duke's Pass

Forest Park, take the **Three Lochs Forest Drive**, which runs for 7 miles, punctuated by picnic spots, hugging the shores of Loch Drunkie and Loch Achray before rejoining the Duke's Pass. **National Cycle Route 7** also meanders northwards from Aberfoyle through the Forest Park, past the David Marshall Lodge and contouring Loch Venachar before reaching Callander. Cycle hire is available locally (☎ 01877 382614; www.trossachscycles.co.uk).

To the east of Aberfoyle, access to the Forest Park is from the **Braevel car park**, where tracks lead onto the Menteith Hills. The hills drop sharply towards Lake of Menteith, and into fields with cup-and-ring-marked stones hiding secrets from a prehistoric past.

The area is now a focus for an ambitious restoration project – the **Great Trossachs Forest**, a plan to create the largest area of natural woodland in Europe. Incorporating the RSPB reserve at Inversnaid and the Woodland Trust land at Glen Finglas, this visionary scheme will plant new trees right at the heart of the National Park and reinforce the existing areas of important woodland on the shores of Loch Lomond.

THE ROAD TO INVERSNAID

The road west of Aberfoyle was made famous by Queen Victoria, who travelled to Stronachlachar with Prince Albert to open the waterworks at Loch Katrine in 1859. Black-and-white painted iron milestones erected specially to commemorate the occasion still line the route like spectators. It is very much a journey into the wild interior of the National Park. A mile west of Aberfoyle is Loch Ard, guarded at its entrance by the hamlet of **Milton**. In her visit in 1859, Queen Victoria stopped at the loch and made a sketch of Ben Lomond. It remains a popular place for walking today – either in Loch Ard Forest or to climb Ben Venue. At the western end of the loch is **Kinlochard**, where there is a shop and café as well as places to stay.

Beyond Kinlochard the scenery becomes wilder, passing Loch Chon towards Loch Arklet. Here the loch has been dammed and water flows into Loch Katrine as part of the scheme to supply Glasgow with water. The road forks at Loch Arklet. Travelling east follows Queen Victoria's route to **Stronachlachar** and the northern terminus of the ss *Sir Walter Scott*. Here, the steamer sets off for Trossachs Pier. This road has been trod not only by Queen Victoria, but also by thousands of her subjects travelling the Trossachs Tour between Inversnaid and Callander or Aberfoyle. Heading west the road descends steeply towards **Inversnaid** and Loch Lomond against the dramatic distant backdrop of the Arrochar Alps.

Mileposts on the road to Stronachlachar,
erected to commemorate the visit of
Queen Victoria in 1859

LOCH KATRINE

Trossachs Trundler calls at Loch Katrine during the summer [☎] 08707 200628
Sailing on Loch Katrine – Loch Katrine Experience [☎] 01877 332000;
www.lochkatrine.com
Cycle hire – Katrinewheelz [☎] 01877 376316; www.lochkatrine.com.

When William and Dorothy Wordsworth walked up Loch Katrine on a
rainy day in August 1803, it would have been a different place to today.
Although there would probably have been a rough cart track through
the woods to the loch, there would have been none of the development
which greets the modern visitor. In her journal Dorothy described the
'solitary wildness of Loch Ketterine'.

Although tourists were visiting the loch by the end of the eighteenth
century, Sir Walter Scott's work hugely accelerated its popularity.
Steamships took over from rowing boats in ferrying passengers to
Stronachlachar when the *Gipsy* first set sail in 1843; the ss *Sir Walter*

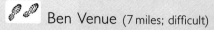

Ben Venue (7 miles; difficult)

The outline of **Ben Venue** dominates the southern shore of Loch Katrine and forms the backdrop to views up Loch Achray. Sir Walter Scott may not have climbed it, but he did immortalise it in his poem *The Lady of the Lake*, when he wrote:

> High on the south, huge Ben Venue
> Down on the Lake in masses threw
> Crags, knolls and mounds confusedly hurl'd
> The fragments of an earlier world.

The easiest route up the mountain starts from the Forestry Commission car park at Creag Noran, north of Loch Achray Hotel (buses from Callander and Aberfoyle stop at the hotel). From the car park, head west into Achray Forest following the forest road until it joins the Ben Venue hill path at Gleann Riabhach. The path contours round the south of the hill and reaches the summit from the west, with spectacular views of Loch Katrine. The path surface is generally firm though there are sections which are uneven and wet underfoot. If you are planning to walk this route ensure that you have strong footwear, waterproofs and extra warm clothing with you. Allow at least six hours.

Scott, which plies the waters today, was the most recent having been brought into service in 1900.

Glasgow's need for clean water had a profound affect on the landscape. In 1838 and 1846 cholera outbreaks swept through the city. In response Glasgow Corporation drew up plans to extract 200 million litres of water a day from the loch. The original aqueduct, which carried the water 40 kilometres underground to a storage reservoir at Milngavie, was a feat of Victorian engineering sufficiently impressive to bring Queen Victoria herself to open the works in 1859. The network has now been expanded to include Loch Arklet and Glen Finglas reservoir.

There are pluses and minuses to this corporate takeover of Loch Katine. The 8-mile loch now holds some of the cleanest water in Scotland, restricted motorised access to the shore means no developments mar the landscape and the round loch road constructed by the Corporation makes a tranquil route for anyone wishing to explore the area either on foot or by bike. You can hire bikes at Trossachs Pier, book a place on the ferry to Stronachlachar and cycle back, or simply stroll through the lush, mossy oak woods which hug the shore, with plenty of places to picnic.

Cycle trailers at Loch Katrine

However, the grafting of a water supply onto the natural beauty of the loch has changed its sense of place. The 'lonely delight of nature' Dorothy Wordsworth described has been diminished. **Ellen's Isle**, where the lady of Sir Walter Scott's lake lived, is much smaller than in Scott's time. At the head of the loch is **Glengyle**, birthplace of Rob Roy MacGregor. Strath Gartney was part of the MacGregor clan's homeland. **MacGregor burial grounds** can still be found south of Portnellan and further north at Glengyle, but the creation of the reservoir changed many sites with clan tales to tell. Ancient shielings and cattle rustling haunts have been submerged. Eilean Dharag, the **Factor's Island**, the walls of which are visible from Stronachlachar Pier, is now much smaller than in the past. It was here that Rob Roy imprisoned the Duke of Montrose's agent and rent collector, John Graham, for a week during the Jacobite uprisings.

Yet the loch still has a wealth of interest to offer the visitor and many historic places are within walking distance, like the Bealach nam Bo – 'the **Pass of the Cattle**'. Lying at the foot of Ben Venue, it was through here that stolen cattle were reputedly driven. The pass can be reached by the path leading westwards from the Loch Katrine road. Below it is Coire na Uruisgean – 'the **Cave of the Goblins**' – which legend says is haunted by the goblins and elves expelled from the shores of the Lake of Menteith by the prior of Inchmahome. Some say that when a

Park People – Sir Walter Scott

ss *Sir Walter Scott*

Although born and educated in Edinburgh, rural life was never far from Sir Walter Scott's mind. He had spent time in the Borders as a child seeking a cure for his lameness and went regularly to stay in the Highlands. No doubt listening to legends and stories of Reivers and Highlanders sparked his literary imagination. A trained lawyer, he started writing at the age of 25. His first publication in 1796, a collection of rhyming ballads translated from German, couldn't have been more removed from the Trossachs. It was another 14 years before he published *The Lady of the Lake*, the first of four works set in the area and one which made both him and the Trossachs a household name.

The Lady of the Lake was written on a family holiday at Loch Katrine, an epic poem telling a romantic tale of adventure in medieval times and set against the backdrop of the loch. It was a phenomenal success. The first edition of 2,000 barely touched the shelves and four further editions totalling more than 20,000 copies were printed within a year. By 1836 more then 50,000 copies had been sold.

Although he spent much of his adult life at his home at Abbotsford House, near Melrose, the landscape and legends of the Trossachs continued to draw him. Published in 1817, his novel *Rob Roy* was set in the land where the real Rob Roy MacGregor lived just out of reach of the law, rustling livestock and achieving infamy. It was met with critical acclaim and insatiable demand. The initial printing of 10,000 copies was snapped up and a reprint of 3,000 was needed within the first fortnight. Not only did it help to cement Scott's reputation as a writer, it reinforced the Trossachs as a must-see destination on the Romantic literature trail and embedded Roy Rob firmly in the heart of Scottish folklore.

Scott put the Trossachs on the map because he used real place-names in his writing. The Victorian yearning for Romanticism combined with their newly found desire to travel led to an explosion of tourists visiting the Trossachs, anxious to taste the scenes Scott described. Some even believed his fiction was fact. The Trossachs was close to home too: travellers could get from Glasgow or Edinburgh to Callander or Aberfoyle by train, then take a horse coach to Loch Katrine for a cruise on the loch and still be home in time for tea.

After *A Legend of Montrose* was published in 1819, Scott did not write about the area again before his death 13 years later. He spent his last decade frantically writing his way out of business debt. By then the stories Scott had penned about the Trossachs were indelibly etched on the cultural landscape of the National Park.

Places to visit associated with Sir Walter Scott:

Aberfoyle – Scott spent time writing *Rob Roy* at the Old Manse and scenes from the novel are set here.

Loch Katrine – Setting of Scott's famous *The Lady of the Lake*.

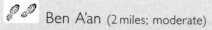 Ben A'an (2 miles; moderate)

What **Ben A'an** lacks in size it makes up for in stature. Sitting like a pimple on the otherwise featureless face of Meall Gainmheich at the eastern end of Loch Katrine, Ben A'an offers a panorama disproportionate to the effort involved in reaching its summit. It is best climbed from the path opposite the Forestry Commission Scotland's car park west of the Tigh Mor.

The distinctive peak of Ben A'an

The path climbs steeply through woods until the impressive summit of Ben A'an is displayed ahead. Soon the path diverges. The left route is for climbers heading towards the steep outcrops and small cliffs on the south face. Continue around the back of the cone to reach the summit from the north and enjoy magnificent panoramic views out over Loch Katrine, Loch Achray and the summit of Ben Venue. The return trip is less than 2 miles.

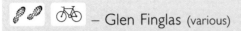 – Glen Finglas (various)

www.glen-finglas.info

Barely visible from the road, Glen Finglas stretches out for 5 miles north of **Brig o' Turk** – 'the Bridge of the Boar', built in 1796. Access to the glen is either on trails leading from Brig o' Turk itself, where there are also refreshments, or from the Woodland Trust's Glen Finglas car park east of the village. It was once a hunting forest of Stewart kings and queens, and the landscape inspired Sir Walter Scott's ballad 'Glenfinlas'. Shielings along the burn side in Gleann Casaig and at the head of the loch also reflect a time when the glen was more widely used than today.

The glen was dammed in 1955 to supply water to Glasgow as part of the network which included Loch Katrine, via a pipeline under Ben A'an. Since acquiring the glen in 1996, the Woodland Trust is restoring the glen's ancient woodland, one of the largest collections of ancient trees in Scotland. Cycling and walking trails of different lengths tour the glen, including a challenging 15-mile circuit and a path that leads over to Balquhidder.

local virgin spurned a goblin's advances, he caused a nearby fountain to overflow and she drowned in the loch that was formed, and the loch now bears her name.

Loch Venachar

Loch Venachar dominates the approach to Callander and provides opportunities for sailing, fishing, walking, cycling and birdwatching. The loch is rich in native species of fish including brown trout, sea trout, pike and salmon. It is also home to rare varieties of lamprey. The clean waters of the river Teith and its tributaries are ideal for this vicious predator. Using their suction-cup-like mouths they attach themselves to the skin of a fish, rasping away tissue with their sharp probing tongue and teeth. Secretions in the lamprey's mouth prevent the victim's blood from clotting, leaving them to die from blood loss or infection.

Loch Venachar's important ecology means access is restricted, particularly in the Blackwater Marshes area during the breeding season. However, boat hire and fly-fishing permits are available from **Venachar Lochside** (📞 01877 330011; www.venachar-lochside.co.uk), where there is also a café. Sailing is available at the Loch Venachar Sailing Club (📞 01324 712892; www.loch-venachar-sc.org.uk) on the south shore. There are footpaths along the southern shore and in Little Drum Wood, which is part of the Woodland Trust for Scotland's land at Glen Finglas. The path through the woods leads to views across Blackwater Marshes – a good place for watching wintering and breeding wildfowl and wading birds. National Cycle Route 7 also runs south of the loch.

On the slopes of Ben Ledi, at the eastern tip of the loch is **Dunmore Fort**. Native woodland is being regenerated on the land by the Woodland Trust for Scotland as part of the Great Trossachs Forest. This prehistoric fort probably dates back 2,000 years and lies on a prominent hill overlooking Callander. It was defended by walls covering all sides except the east where steep slopes provided sufficient defence. Access to this Iron Age settlement is via a short path leading from the road.

Callander

Buses connect Callander with Stirling
Information centre 📞 08707 200628; **www.incallander.co.uk**

Arriving from the wild glens and lonely lochs of the Trossachs, Callander has an almost cosmopolitan feel. Its wide streets and broad central square give the town a sense of space. There is an eclectic mix of building styles, notably the turreted frontage of the Dreadnought Hotel, the slender Gothic spires of the old St Kessog's Church, and the pink-hued, former eighteenth-century hunting lodge of the Roman Camp Hotel. A stroll round the town is like walking through an architectural textbook.

Callander's urban style is both a cultural and physical by-product of the Highland Boundary Fault. Prior to the Jacobite rebellions of 1715 and 1745 the town was nothing more than a cluster of crofters' cottages. This changed with the arrival of Major Caulfeild's military road in 1743. The road, connecting Stirling with the garrison at Fort William, was part of government plans to pacify the Highlanders, and along with the road came a new town. Plans for a settlement had been drawn up

Callander main street

in the 1730s by the local laird, James Drummond, the Duke of Perth. However, his family had sided with the defeated Bonnie Prince Charlie at Culloden in 1746 and their property had been confiscated by the Crown as a result. Not only did the government steal his land, they stole his idea too, seeing a new town into which rebellious clansmen could be settled as an ideal way to calm the storm blowing across the Highland–Lowland divide.

In this way Callander became one of Scotland's first planned towns. Squeezed between the abrupt slopes of Callander Crags, thrown upwards by the Fault, and the waters of the river Teith, there was little choice other than to realise Drummond's original plan for a tight grid pattern of roads and houses. Walk down Callander's spacious Main Street towards the visitor information centre in Ancaster Square, crossed by its broad east–west roads, and you are following a route that was laid down by post-Jacobean planners more than 250 years ago.

Over the next century the town was transformed into a busy gateway to the Trossachs. In 1818, barely half a century after it was built, the poet John Keats was already describing the town as being 'vexatiously full of visitors'. Fifty years later the railway arrived, cementing Callander's reputation as a tourist destination. This has remained despite the demise of the railway, which now doubles up as the Rob Roy Way and National Cycle Route 7.

Unfortunately, in their haste to get to Killin and beyond, the Victorians drove the railway line right across the remains of **Bochastle**

Bracklinn Falls (4 miles; moderate)

Bracklinn Falls are a short walk from Callander town centre

A popular trip for Victorians, the walk to **Bracklinn Falls** is easy to do from Callander town centre. The 4-mile walk starts at Bracklinn Road. Walk up the road for quarter of a mile until a track leads to the falls on the right. At the falls cross the bridge onto the east side of the burn and continue along the path north until it meets a minor road. Follow the road towards Callander and take the path under Callander Crags to return to the town.

Roman Fort. Short-lived as a military outpost, the first-century fort was abandoned within a few years along with other encampments north of the Forth–Clyde line, when ambitions to conquer the Scottish Highlands were given up. What remains of the fort can be seen from the old railway half a mile west of the town.

The visitor information centre is located in old St Kessog's Church in Ancaster Square. Kessog also has his own mound in the town, Tom na Chesaig – 'the Hill of Kessog', beside the river Teith off Bridge Street, adjacent to the old parish graveyard, where legend says he used to preach. Further down Main Street is the **Hamilton Toy Collection** (☎ 01877 330004; www.thehamiltontoycollection.co.uk), which claims to be a museum of every toy you can remember: dolls' houses, comic books, Corgi toys, model railways, they are all here.

The town has plenty of shops, cafés, restaurants, pubs and services and **Callander Meadows**, at the west end of town is ideal for a picnic. A mile up the road at Kilmahog are the **Trossachs Woollen Mill** (📞 01877 330178) and **Kilmahog Woollen Mill** (📞 01877 330268), ever popular with coach parties. Callander lies on the National Cycle Route 7 and there are many cycling options nearby. Cycle hire is available from Mounter Bikes (📞 01877 331052; www.callandercyclehire.co.uk) and Wheels Cycle Centre (📞 01877 331100; www.scottish-cycling.com).

LAKE OF MENTEITH AND INCHMAHOME PRIORY

Buses connect Lake of Menteith with Stirling

Three miles east of Aberfoyle is the hamlet of **Port of Menteith**. Although it boasts a Gothic church and Nick Nairn's Cook School, it is the adjacent Lake of Menteith which draws most visitors. This broadly circular stretch of tranquil blue lies at the foot of the Highland Boundary Fault and it has a distinctly lowland feel. Its shoreline reveals a succession of natural habitats and its waters are home to rare plants. In winter pink-footed geese come to feed and you can see heron and ospreys fishing in summer.

It is not only birds that fish the lake – it is regarded as one of the best places for rainbow and brown trout fishing in Scotland. Fishing is closely regulated by the **Lake of Menteith Fisheries** (📞 01877 385664; www.menteith-fisheries.co.uk), from where boats can be hired. A small boat takes you to **Inchmahome Priory** (📞 01877 385294; www.historic-scotland.gov.uk), an isolated Augustinian ruin on the largest of the lake's three islands. The short crossing gives you time to contemplate the lives of the monks who once lived there. It also gives you time to imagine the scene here in February 1979 when an estimated 10,000 spectators watched the last Grand Match to take place on the lake. This great curling contest between the north and south of Scotland can only take place when the lake is frozen to a depth of at least 25cm, something which hasn't happened for over three decades.

All may be peaceful now on Inchmahome, but its history is not without colour. The priory was established around 1238 by a small community of Augustinian canons. Their founder and patron was Walter Comyn, Earl of Menteith, whose residence, now inaccessible and

The Lake of Menteith is popular with fishermen

unrecognisable, stood on the adjacent island of Inch Talla. Robert the Bruce visited three times in the fourteenth century and in 1547 Mary Queen of Scots sought sanctuary here for four weeks until her safe passage to France could be guaranteed. As isolated as the priory is, it still could not avoid the ravages of the Reformation. With the shift in religious power, authority over the priory gradually passed into secular hands and its role declined. It is now managed by Historic Scotland, which runs a small visitor centre on the island.

The imposing frame of the east window gives an idea of the grandeur which the original building would have possessed. The chapter house survives well, having been converted to a mausoleum in the seventeenth century. It now houses a fine collection of carved stones. The tombs of Don Roberto – Robert Cunninghame Graham – and his wife Gabrielle also lie in the grounds. With its mixture of romantic setting and adventurous arrival the priory remains one of the most popular destinations in the Trossachs.

A walk along the short path around the shore can be added to a visit to the priory ruins. From here you can see the Arnmach peninsula, which juts northwards from the southern shore of the lake. Local legend says that it was from here that a prior of Inchmahome banished local fairies and elves to the Cave of the Goblins on Loch Katrine.

Golden eagle – a rare sighting on the Trossachs Bird of Prey Trail

East of Lake of Menteith, just outside the National Park boundary, is **Flanders Moss**. This National Nature Reserve is a spectacular area of lowland bog rich in wildlife, with access and trails for visitors. For more information visit www.nnr-scotland.org.uk.

Trossachs Bird of Prey Trail

www.birdofpreytrail.com

This 40-kilometre circular trail offers good opportunities to see some of Scotland's most spectacular birds. The route cuts through the heart of the Trossachs but can be cycled or accessed using the Trossachs Trundler. It links the David Marshall Lodge visitor centre in Aberfoyle with the **Argaty Red Kites Project** (www.argatyredkites.co.uk) near Doune, which, as central Scotland's only red kite feeding station, is well worth a visit. On the signposted trail are viewpoints, picnic areas, walks and lay-bys. The Lake of Menteith and Loch Venachar are good places to look for ospreys, while at the Duke's Pass, Glen Finglas or Inversnaid you may be lucky enough to see a golden eagle. Much easier to spot are buzzards, kestrels and sparrowhawks hunting around the fields and in woods along the trail.

Opposite: Balquhidder Church

PART FOUR

BREADALBANE

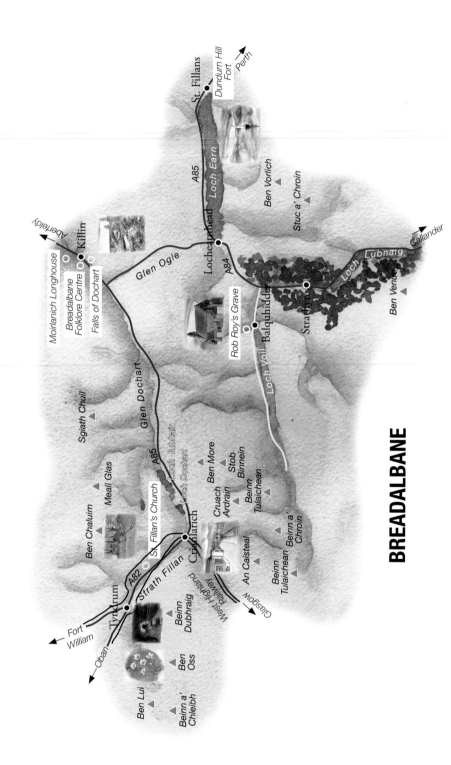

BREADALBANE

Breadalbane

Panorama of Breadalbane

There could hardly be a starker contrast with the picturesque landscape of the Trossachs or the playful shores of Loch Lomond than Breadalbane – the wildest part of the National Park. The word Breadalbane is Gaelic for the 'high country of Scotland' and a more fitting description would be hard to find. Of the National Park's 21 Munros, 16 are in Breadalbane; there is no hint of the Lowlands here. Geology has thrown up these giants, but it has also exposed base-rich rocks which have provided fertile ground for rare alpine flowers on the slopes of Ben Lui, Ben More and, just outside the National Park, on Ben Lawers. Eagles and peregrine falcons soar in the sky and stags roar in the glens. It is no surprise that Breadalbane attracts walkers, climbers and naturalists in their droves.

Yet it has not always been so wild. This area is where Scotland had its origins: in the eighth century the Celtic missionary St Fillan brought Christianity, binding together the Gaels and the Picts and paving the way for a united Scotland. Castles are scattered through the landscape, pointing to a time when feuding clans clashed over power and property. The MacNabs, the MacGregors, the MacNeishes and the Campbells all fought here in the Middle Ages. The Campbells ultimately rose to the top and became the Earls of Breadalbane, lauding their status over the other clans.

The influence of the clans waned after the failure of the Jacobite rebellions. Roads were driven through their territory, followed by railways. The new invaders were Victorians from Glasgow, Edinburgh and further afield and the era of tourism took off. Hotels were built and the stage was set for the Breadalbane of today, where landscape and history are the main attractions.

The Road to Balquhidder Glen

When it comes to communications the Highlands have long presented an obstacle. So it is no surprise to see that the Pass of Leny, a thin glacier-driven slice through the mountains north of Callander, became the route for road and rail favoured by military generals and Victorian engineers alike. Here the river Leny is squeezed out of Loch Lubnaig and tumbles over rocks and down the **Falls of Leny**. The falls can be viewed from the road and there is parking close by.

Balquhidder can be reached following either side of Loch Lubnaig. To the west, National Cycle Route 7 and Rob Roy Way follow the bed of the old Callander and Oban railway. Opened in 1870, and closed following a landslide in 1965, the railway line now offers a spectacular off-road route between Callander and Killin. To the west of the loch the A85 follows the old military road to Fort William, passing the remains of **St Bride's Chapel** before reaching **Loch Lubnaig**.

There are several picnic places along the sinuous Loch Lubnaig before reaching **Strathyre** – 'the valley of the corn land' – reflecting the farming past of this area. The village lies in Strathyre Forest, planted during the 1930s and now part of the Queen Elizabeth Forest Park. You can access the Rob Roy Way from the village and there are waymarked forest walks including the ascent of Beinn an t-Sidhean, which overlooks the glen. The village has a post office and places to eat and drink. Past Strathyre the glen opens out. The entrance to Balquhidder Glen is marked by the Kingshouse Hotel. 'King's House' was a name commonly associated with inns at construction camps on the military roads, but this one was built at the request of drovers who travelled the route on the way to markets at Falkirk.

Balquhidder Glen

The nearest bus stop is the Kingshouse Hotel, with connections to Stirling and Tyndrum. A special taxi service runs in the glen which can be booked at the Kingshouse Hotel and costs the equivalent of a bus fare 01877 384768

Arrive in Balquhidder Glen today and you enter one of the most tranquil and wild parts of the National Park. For seven meandering miles the

Ben Ledi (5 miles; difficult)

The outline of Ben Ledi dominates the view north of Callander and is a popular climb. Its name means 'mountain of the Gods' and, according to tradition, on the summit Druids worshipped Bel, the Celtic god of the sun. The festival of Beltane was celebrated here on May Day with the lighting of a huge bonfire in the hope that summer's light and warmth would bring a good harvest. The only divine aspect of Ben Ledi today is the panoramic view from the top, stretching from the Paps of Jura in the west to Bass Rock in the east on a clear day. The climb to the summit starts from a small parking area just off the A84, reached by a girder bridge across the river just upstream from the Falls of Leny. A well-marked path climbs through trees before joining the south-east ridge rising up to the summit.

The distinctive shape of Ben Ledi rises behind Callander

You can return by the same route or continue north and descend Stank Glen to the old railway line from the macabrely named **Bealach nan Corp** – 'the pass of the corpse'. But take care. Legend has it that on a chill winter's day a burial party from Glen Finglas was crossing the pass en route to the graveyard at St Bride's Chapel in the Pass of Leny. So cold was it that the party decided to take an ill-fated short cut across the nearby frozen loch. Halfway across the ice broke and the party drowned in the freezing water.

narrow road traverses the glen passing the salmon-filled, silken waters of Loch Voil and Loch Doine before ending abruptly at a picnic spot. Beyond here the glen has five more miles to travel before the Bealach nan Corp crosses over into Glengyle and towards Loch Katrine.

With seven Munros bordering the glen this really is the high country of Scotland from which Breadalbane takes its name. Here the mountain dwellers are evocative of wild places: golden eagle, red deer, mountain hare and ptarmigan live on these slopes. The alpine flowers which flourish here are internationally important. This is spectacular walking country with the twin peaks of Ben More and Stob Binnein being the most well-known and recognisable. From their summits you can see both Ben Nevis and Glasgow. The best approach is from Benmore Glen in the north or Inverlochlarig Glen in the south.

The world of the high places is the domain of the experienced hillwalker and most people are content to remain close to **Balquhidder** village. It seems quiet today, but the glen has teemed with life in the past. Nowhere is this more evident than at the top of Glen Buckie, south of Balquhidder, where there is now neither farmstead nor road, yet there is a cluster of 22 ancient shielings dating back to medieval times. And while it is easy to eulogise the natural beauty of the glen you cannot ignore the barbarity of the past which scars the memory of the valley.

A board inside **Balquhidder Church** lists more than 150 surnames associated with the eight clans whose roots are entwined in the history of the glen: MacNabs, MacIntyres, Stewarts, Buchanans, Campbells, Fergusons, MacGregors and MacLarens have all shaped its social tapestry.

The twin peaks of Ben More and Stob Binnein, two of Breadalbane's 16 Munros

Succession between clans was not always harmonious. One dark night in 1558 the MacGregors came over the hills from Glen Dochart and burnt eighteen MacLaren households, virtually wiping out a clan which had had a presence in the glen for more than 300 years.

The MacGregors were the most notorious of the clans, who better than any knew the meaning of the phrase 'fire and sword' as it was enacted both by them and on them. Perhaps the worst crime accredited to the clan came in 1559 when some MacGregors were caught poaching by the king's forester, John Drummond. The ringleaders were executed on the spot, as was the law for anyone robbing the monarch of game; others were sent home minus their ears to teach their fellow clansman a lesson. Unfortunately it didn't work. Instead vengeance bred vengeance and the MacGregors responded by hunting down the forester and cutting off his head. They wrapped it in a plaid and made their way to Ardvorlich House on Loch Earn, where the forester's sister was married to the Stewart laird. They asked for hospitality and were given bread and cheese. When Lady Stewart entered the room she found her brother's bloody head in the centre of the table with bread and cheese stuffed into his mouth.

The MacGregors fled with their gory trophy to Balquhidder where the clan chief's brother had a stronghold at the foot of Loch Voil. In a macabre ceremony the severed head was placed on the altar of the ancient church and the clansmen walked up, placed their hands on the head and swore to protect the murderers. There was no happy ending: the clan chief Alistair MacGregor and 130 of his fellow clansmen were proscribed, that is put outside the protection of the law. If caught, their lands were sold and the proceeds shared between the Crown and those who caught them; anyone hunting MacGregors was exonerated of blame regarding what might happen to clan members if they got caught. The clan was persecuted like this until a pardon was granted in 1596. There is a MacGregor burial ground at the foot of Loch Doine and many clan graves lie in the churchyard, including, later, the tomb of Rob Roy.

There has been a church in Balquhidder for 800 years, and ceremonies for much longer. As on nearby Ben Ledi, Druids worshipped Bel on the knoll behind the current church. Christianity was brought by St Angus, a monk from Dunblane in the eighth century and the first church was supposedly built over his grave 500 years later. A second church was built on the same site in 1631. This was where the MacGregors swore their murderous vows and where Rev. Robert Kirk preached for 20 years before moving on to Aberfoyle and encountering fairies. Its ruins stand in the graveyard. The current church, built in 1855, was a gift from local businessman David Carnegie who owned nearby Stronvar House. There

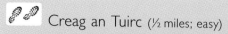

Creag an Tuirc (½ miles; easy)

To escape from the grisly tales of internecine clans take a short walk from Balquhidder Church through Forestry Commission Scotland woodland to **Creag an Tuirc** – 'the boar's rock', following the trail alongside the church. This was the traditional meeting place of the MacLaren clan and offers spectacular views up the glen and into Glen Buckie.

is a small exhibition of the church's history inside as well as the stone reputed to have covered St Angus' tomb.

LOCH EARN TO ST FILLANS

Buses connect Lochearnhead with Stirling, Callander and Tyndrum
St Fillans has regular connections from Perth and a daily bus from Lochearnhead

Loch Earn points eastwards out of the National Park like a long, narrow finger. It shares with Lake Geneva, Lake Erie, Lake Garda and Lake Baikal an unusual watery phenomenon – that of an apparent tidal oscillation or 'seiche' caused by the action of the wind blowing along the loch. The combination of its east–west orientation and the prevailing wind direction causes the water level to build up at one end of the loch. Over time this applied pressure can result in an oscillation and the water returns to the opposite end of the loch. In the case of Loch Earn, this is a period of 16 hours and although the effect can be measured, it is difficult to observe.

Water-based activities are central to Loch Earn. Fishing is popular and permits are available from Lochearnhead post office. Lochearnhead Watersports (☎ 01567 830330; www.lochearnhead-water-sports.co.uk) offers water skiing and canoeing, and sailing facilities are available at Loch Earn Sailing Club (www.lochearnsc.com). **Lochearnhead** village at the western end of the loch has hotels, shops and a post office. Today it is the junction of two roads, but in the past it was railways which met here with a branch line towards St Fillans and Crieff joining the Callander and Oban railway. At the south-east corner of the loch is Edinample Castle; the castle was built by 'Black' Duncan Campbell on land taken after the proscription of the MacGregors in the sixteenth century. Unfortunately there is no public access.

At the eastern end of Loch Earn is **St Fillans**. Built in the nineteenth

Loch Earn is a popular centre for sailing and watersports

century, it still retains much of its Victorian grandeur. A short distance from the village on a path through the golf course is **St Fillan's Chapel**, the burial ground of the Stewarts of Ardvorlich. It is overlooked by **Dundurn Hill Fort**. This Pictish fort from the eighth century would have provided a fine defensive position at the end of Loch Earn and its extensive views can still be enjoyed today.

KILLIN

Buses connect Killin with Stirling, Callander, Tyndrum and Aberfeldy
Information centre 📞 08707 200627; www.killin.co.uk

The most dramatic point of entry into Killin is down the long sweeping arc of **Glen Ogle**, either along the old military road or the old Callander and Oban railway line. Magnificent Highland scenery is all around Killin, which serves as the eastern gateway to the National Park. Few can be left unimpressed by the sweeping **Falls of Dochart** which mark the entrance to the village. On a summer day the exposed rocks over which the river Dochart weaves its path are a favourite picnic spot.

Killin is steeped in legend, the story of which is told at the **Breadalbane Folk Centre** (📞 01567 820254; www.breadalbanefolklorecentre.com), housed in an old water mill next to the falls; it is also the tourist

Falls of Dochart, Killin

information centre. The village takes its name from the Celtic folk hero Fingal, who tradition maintains is buried here. A short path from the main street leads to a small standing stone, known as Fingal's Stone, which is believed to mark his grave. The Celtic missionary St Fillan, who travelled throughout Breadalbane, is also remembered in the village: one of the oldest Celtic fonts in the Highlands, and the only seven-sided font in Scotland, can be found in the parish church at the north end of the village.

But it is the clans who have stamped their mark indelibly on the village. If you are a MacNab, then Killin is your traditional homeland, for the clan has lived in these parts for 800 years. Opposite the Falls of Dochart on an island on the river is the MacNab burial ground. If you want to visit, keys are available from the visitor information centre, where you can also find out about the stone circle on the island. The MacNabs were a hardy, warlike clan, who fought many battles, particularly against the neighbouring MacNeishes.

This story, from the seventeenth century when the last remnants of the MacNeish clan were living on an island on Loch Earn, is perhaps the best known. One Christmas the chief of MacNabs sent his servant to Crieff for provisions. However, on his return the servant was attacked and robbed of all he had. He survived and returned empty-handed to the MacNab chief. The chief had twelve sons; the strongest of them was known as 'Smooth' John MacNab. He and his brothers set out over the mountains carrying a fishing boat on their shoulders. They arrived at Loch Earn where they launched the boat and sailed over to MacNeish Island. On arrival Smooth John MacNab kicked open the door of the MacNeishes' house, taking the MacNeishes by surprise and then set about killing them. Only one MacNeish, a boy, survived by hiding under a bed. The MacNabs returned, carrying off the heads of the MacNeishes and any plunder they could secure.

Whatever the MacNabs could do, their successors, the Campbells, could do better, particularly 'Black' Duncan Campbell, perhaps the most ruthless of the Campbell clan. It was Black Duncan who was most enthusiastic about stamping out the MacGregor name following King James' order that the clan should be eradicated after the battle of Glen Fruin. Obsessed with power, he built or improved seven houses on his estate (so prolific was he at building that he was known as 'Black Duncan of Seven Castles'), including **Finlarig Castle** a short walk north of the village centre. Sadly the castle is now in ruins and dangerous, but near the castle's north wall you can still see the stone-lined pit which, legend has it, was used for beheading prisoners of noble blood. Commoners were hanged on a nearby oak tree.

One mile north of Killin, with a less murderous history, is **Moirlanich Longhouse** (www.nts.org.uk). This National Trust for Scotland property is open to the public. It is a rare example of the Scottish longhouse, a type of building in which a family and their livestock lived under one roof. This longhouse, with many original features intact, dates from at least the mid nineteenth century and was built from locally available materials – timber, stone, clay, sand, turf and bracken.

Killin village has plenty of shops and places to eat and stay as well as an outdoor centre where Canadian canoes can be hired (☎ 01567 820652; www.killinoutdoor.co.uk). There are a number of walks of varying difficulty and a leaflet is available from the tourist information centre, where information on fishing permits for the area can also be obtained. **Ben Lawers National Nature Reserve** (www.nnr-scotland.org.uk) – a challenging Munro also famous for its mountain flowers – can be visited 2 miles west of Killin just outside the National Park on the shores of Loch Tay.

Glen Dochart

Glen Dochart runs for 15 miles between Killin and Crianlarich. Rising up each side are some of the highest mountains in the National Park including a number of Munros. Few people live in the glen today, but in the past MacNabs, MacGregors and Campbells have all held power here. St Fillan built his priory at Suie. There are ancient burial grounds at Suie and Auchlyne. On an island on **Loch Dochart** are the inaccessible remains of one of Black Duncan Campbell's castles. Dorothy Wordsworth, on her visit to Scotland in 1803, described it as 'a place of retirement and peace', but it is unlikely to have been so in bloodthirsty Black Duncan's time. There is a parking place at neighbouring Loch Lubhair, and a lay-by by Loch Dochart, from where you can watch wintering wildfowl. Several paths lead from the glen into the mountains and over to Balquhidder.

The West Highland Railway at Crianlarich

CRIANLARICH

Buses connect Crianlarich to Glasgow, Edinburgh, Stirling, Callander, Fort William and Oban
Trains connect Crianlarich to Glasgow, Oban and Fort William

Crianlarich is a natural crossroads. Its name in Gaelic means 'the low pass' and it has long been a place travellers journey through. In the eighteenth century it was at the meeting of two military roads, one south through Glen Falloch to Dumbarton and one east to Callander and Stirling. The two routes joined at Crianlarich and headed north to Fort William. In the nineteenth century the railways arrived following the same route, although now only one line, the West Highland Railway, runs through the village; its station has one of the finest views of any. Now the A82 and A85 follow almost the same route as the original military roads.

The West Highland Way passes through the village and with more than a dozen Munros within 10 miles of the village. Crianlarich is a popular haunt for hillwalkers, offering a real taste of Highland scenery. For the less energetic there is a short woodland walk running through the **Crianlarich Community Woodland**, starting from the car park at the east end of the village. Long accustomed to visitors, accommodation in Crianlarich is plentiful, with hotels, B&Bs, campsites and a youth hostel; there is also a shop, post office and places to eat.

Strathfillan

Strathfillan runs north of Crianlarich towards Tyndrum. Surrounded by some of the highest mountains in the National Park, it is the main route for road and rail and also offers some good walks.

The majestic red deer roams in Breadalbane

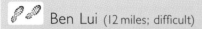 Ben Lui (12 miles; difficult)

www.nnr-scotland.org.uk

An ascent of **Ben Lui** can also be made from Dalrigh car park. This spectacular Munro is the highest and most famous of a cluster of four Munros in the north-west corner of the National Park. The mountain appeals not only to hillwalkers and climbers, but also to naturalists too. The Ben Lui range of peaks is designated as a National Nature Reserve. Its moist cliffs and rocky outcrops support an unusually lush growth of mountain plants, thriving on soils that are less acid than elsewhere. Beautiful saxifrages and rich carpets of mosses and lichens are its speciality.

The five radiating ridges of Ben Lui are best appreciated by approaching from the east, starting from Tyndrum Lower station or Dalrigh. Tracks from both starting points merge and follow Glen Cononish to the foot of Ben Lui. From here the route follows the northern ridge of the mountain to the summit. Ben Lui is a big mountain, the fifteenth highest in Britain, and care needs to be taken when climbing it whatever the time of year.

 Strathfillan woodlands (various)

Almost opposite Auchtertyre at **Dalrigh** is the **Tyndrum Community Woodland**. A short walk in native woodlands recently planted by the Tyndrum community starts from the car park in an old quarry. There are good views of the surrounding mountains and sculptures on this easy walk which takes in the riverside and can be started from, or extended to, Tyndrum, where there is public transport access by following the West Highland Way south from the village.

It was here at the Battle of Dalrigh that Robert the Bruce suffered one of his rare defeats in the summer of 1306. His forces found themselves outnumbered by the MacDougalls of Argyll, allies of the English, who were seeking vengeance for Bruce's murder of their kinsman John Comyn. Local tradition says that in his haste to retreat following the defeat, to lighten his load Bruce threw his sword into **Lochan nan Arm** – 'the lochan of the lost sword' – and it is still there to this day. The lochan is a short walk from the car park. Continuing past Lochan nan Arm the path enters **Coille Coire Chuilc woodland**. This is the most southerly extensive remnant of the ancient Caledonian pinewood which once covered much of northern Scotland. Here Scots pines grow with birch and rowan in one of the most important areas of native woodland in the National Park.

Auchtertyre Farm (various)

01838 400251; **www.sac.ac.uk**

Managed by the Scottish Agricultural College, **Auchtertyre Farm** is signposted as Strathfillan Wigwams from the A85. These can be rented if you want accommodation with a difference. The college has also created an excellent range of walks of varying difficulty and there are picnic areas and a farm shop. Walks are colour-coded and easy to follow, offering moorland tracks visiting ancient shielings, a stroll down to St Fillan's Holy Pool, or a route downriver to St Fillan's Church. Foxes, deer, golden eagles, otters, owls, dragonflies and butterflies can all be seen on walks from the farm.

Park People – St Fillan

St Fillan's Church

St Fillan came from good Celtic stock. An Irish Celt, his mother was St Kentigerna, who lived and died on Inchcailloch on Loch Lomond. He came north to Breadalbane in the eighth century and spread Christianity throughout the district. His name is associated with the glen that runs between Crianlarich and Tyndrum and its rivers, as well as a number of other sites in Breadalbane. Although the remains of his chapel are in Strathfillan, the saint founded his monastery in Glen Dochart at Suie. Its most famous guest and the saint's biggest fan was Robert the Bruce. He took refuge in the region after being defeated by the English at the Battle of Methven in 1306.

Beaten and bedraggled, Robert the Bruce looked to the cult of the saint to inspire him. St Fillan had a powerful influence over King Robert, and when he miraculously escaped from his enemies, the MacDougalls, at the Battle of Dalrigh, near Tyndrum, it was to the saint he gave thanks. So obsessed was he with the saint that he had his priest bring the saint's embalmed arm to Bannockburn in a silver case. The night before the battle, the king was praying to God and St Fillan when a crack was heard in the case. When his priest opened the case he was amazed to find the arm inside, as he confessed to having brought an empty case to the battlefield for fear of losing the prized relic. Buoyed by the miracle, King Robert slept content, assured of the victory which, indeed, he achieved. This was not the only miracle associated with the saint's limb. During St Fillan's lifetime it was said that the saint would spend his time translating the scriptures in his darkened cell illuminated by light emanating from his arm.

Robert the Bruce was one of many believers in the healing power of the saint's relics. In the eighteenth century, if you were insane, bathing in Holy Pool at Strathfillan was about your only hope. Some came from 30 miles away to be lowered by a rope into the sacred waters of St Fillan. Then they were taken a mile south to St Fillan's Church where they were tied to the church font and made to spend the night with St Fillan's bell on their head. By the morning, if they were free, it was said that it was the saint who had cured them from their madness and released them. If they remained tied, then they were said to still be insane, no doubt more so from the ordeal.

Sacred water, magic bells and luminous limbs are only some of the religious paraphernalia which have been associated with St Fillan though the ages. His relics are as venerated as the man himself. Soon after his death a number of artefacts associated with the saint were passed into the keeping of hereditary guardians in and around Glen Dochart, known locally as *deoradh*. Over time the custodian's job became his family name and for centuries Dewars in Glen Dochart were the keepers of the relics of St Fillan. It was a good job, as it brought with it rent-free land courtesy of the king. Over the centuries the relics changed from being symbols of office to objects of awe and superstition, with power to cure the sick; an oath sworn on a relic was as serious a statement as anyone could make. It isn't surprising, then, that custodianship brought with it the wrath of the established church, which wanted to wrest the relics from the dynasty of the Dewars and even challenged their office in the sixteenth century.

There were five relics. The arm was kept by a family in Killin, but was lost at the time of the Reformation. The Dewars of the bell lived at Suie where it was being used for healing at St Fillan's Priory up until the eighteenth century, when it was stolen by an Englishman who took it to Hertfordshire. The bell was eventually recovered and can be seen today at the National Museum of Scotland. Details of two other relics, the 'meser' and the the 'fergy', are more sketchy and no one seems to know what these were or what happened to them. The fergy, thought to be a stone or a shrine, was preserved in a chapel, the remains of which still stand in a field between Auchlyne and the river Dochart. Perhaps the most famous of St Fillan's relics is his crozier or staff, with its ornately-fashioned handle and casing of silver, bronze and copper. It is a well-travelled crook, having been finally brought back to Scotland from Canada in 1877. Like the bell, it is on display at the National Museum of Scotland.

Breadalbane Folklore Centre, Killin

At Killin, the Breadalbane Folklore Centre is said to stand on the site of a mill erected by the saint himself. Close by there was a seat where he sat and preached under a large ash tree. In the eighteenth century the seat was washed away by a flood and the tree blew down in a gale. But until then both were treated as sacred by the people of Killin. An irreverent local who dared to lop off a branch of the tree found his house burned down soon afterwards. Inside the centre you can still see St Fillan's healing stones – eight highly polished rocks of different sizes and shapes, each associated with different parts of the body and bestowed with healing power. Up to the nineteenth century an old woman lived rent-free in the village in return for administering cures with the stones.

Places to visit associated with St Fillan:

Holy Pool – The Saint's healing pool in Strathfillan at Auchtertyre.

St Fillan's Church, Kirkton – The remains of a church dedicated to the saint.

St Fillan's Seat, Suie, Glen Dochart – The site of the saint's monastery. There are no remains, but an ancient burial ground by the river Dochart has a Latin cross which may go back to St Fillan.

Auchlyne – The remains of the chapel of the fergy.

Breadalbane Folklore Centre, Killin – St Fillan's healing stones and mill.

Tyndrum

Buses connect Tyndrum to Glasgow, Dumbarton, Edinburgh, Stirling, Callander, Fort William and Oban
Trains connect Tyndrum to Glasgow, Oban and Fort William
Information centre 08707 200626

Tyndrum lies at the northern gateway to the National Park and there is the sense of a frontier about the village. The village receives many passing travellers. Its hotels, petrol station, cafés and two railway stations aid not only travellers to the area but those going onwards to Fort William and to Oban for it is a village where routes divide north and

Mining at Tyndrum

west. Its railways are an anomaly: two stations serving the same relatively small community, separated physically by only a few hundred yards, but about 5 miles apart by rail. This reflects the history of the railways in the area and the two uncooperative railway companies that built separate lines through the village, rather than working together.

On the hill west of the village a path leads away to the **Tyndrum lead mines**. Long forgotten as an industry, lead mining at Tyndrum began in the mid eighteenth century and continued intermittently until 1858 by which time several thousand tonnes of lead ore had been recovered. The veins had been mined to a depth of 230 metres and the last attempt to re-open the mines was in the early 1920s. The shafts are sealed now, but you can visit the site, or go on a guided walk in the area. Three miles south of Tyndrum is the UK's last gold mine at Cononish, where there are long-term plans to open the mine again. The West Highland Way passes through the village and a short Forestry Commission Scotland walk begins in the village, following an ancient drover's road through woodland behind Tyndrum Lower station.

Opposite: The Cobbler

PART FIVE

ARGYLL FOREST AND
THE ARROCHAR ALPS

Inveraray

Glen Kinglas

Ben Vane

Ardkinglas
Gardens

Beinn Ime

Ben Narnain

Loch Fyne

A815

Hell's Glen

Rest and be
thankful

The Cobbler

Glen Croe

Glen Loin

Tarbet

A83

Ardgartan
Visitor Centre

Arrochar

Strachur

Lochgoilhead

Argyll
Forest Park

Loch Goil

Glenbranter

Castle
Carrick

Loch Eck

Ben More

**ARGYLL
FOREST**

Ardentinny

Benmore Botanic
Garden

Loch
Long

Kilmun
Church

Blairmore

Kilmun

Strone

Holy Loch

Sandbank

Dunoon

The Argyll Forest and the Arrochar Alps

Panorama of the Argyll Forest

The quarter of the National Park which encompasses the Argyll Forest stretches from the Arrochar Alps at the head of Loch Long to Holy Loch north of Dunoon. It covers the northern half of the Cowal peninsula. Although Cowal extends beyond the National Park, a section of the peninsula's coast lies within the park boundary and adds a different dimension, with its sea lochs and sandy beaches. Its closeness to the sea gives the area of the National Park which covers the Argyll Forest an atmosphere quite distinct from the high places of Breadalbane or the lochs of the Trossachs.

It was from Loch Long that the Vikings invaded Loch Lomond in the thirteenth century. King Haakon of Norway dispatched a flotilla of 60 longships to the area in 1263 during a raid on the Scottish coast. The narrow strip of land between Arrochar and Tarbet was no obstacle to the Norsemen, who simply dragged their boats across the isthmus onto Loch Lomond. Then they set about ravaging the shoreline settlements and islands as well as devastating the religious centres on Inchcailloch and Inchtavannach. But it was not all plain sailing for the Viking raiders. Ten ships were wrecked in a storm as they sailed to rejoin the main fleet and King Haakon's men got their comeuppance soon after at the Battle of Largs.

As with the rest of Argyll, the history of this area is linked with Clan Campbell, one of the largest and most powerful of the Highland clans. There are several branches of the clan, including those who moved into Breadalbane. Allies of Robert the Bruce, they were established in Argyll

The Argyll Forest is a great place for seeing red squirrels

during the thirteenth century. So successful, and ruthless, were they that they were eventually elevated to Earls and finally Dukes of Argyll. The Duke of Argyll was one of the most important political figures in Scotland during the sixteenth, seventeenth and eighteenth centuries and remains one of the largest landowners in the region. Some met premature ends, the 8th and 9th earls were executed for treason during the seventeenth century. As with other Highland clan histories their tale is peppered with bloody feuds with neighbouring clans and there is plenty of evidence to support the old Gaelic saying, 'As long as there are trees in the woods there will be treachery in the Campbells'.

Today this part of Argyll is the stronghold of the red squirrel, which has made its home among the tall pines that are hostile to the grey squirrel. The Argyll Forest was the first forest park to be created in the UK. Impenetrable stands of conifers hug the shorelines and lower slopes. Mist swirls among the branches in a landscape resembling the great temperate forests of North America. As well as incorporating woodland, the park includes the Cobbler, one of the most popular mountains in Scotland. The Argyll Forest Park was established by the Forestry Commission in 1935 as the lungs of Glasgow, whose city workers came by steamer or train at weekends and holidays to walk and climb.

The natural beauty of its rugged hills and long fjord-like lochs make the Argyll Forest as popular today. Here is a place to enjoy walking, cycling, horse-riding and fishing or simply picnicking on the loch shores.

The saltwater shores of Loch Long

Although much of the forest comprises new plantings of conifers for the intensive, industrial cycle of harvesting and replanting, there are pockets of important ancient woodland in Hell's Glen and Glen Finart. Argyll's mild climate makes it ideal for growing exotic species and in Benmore and Kilmun you can see trees from around the world. From the top of Beinn Narnain, a lofty Munro overlooking Loch Long, to the lapping waves on the shore at Ardentinny, the Argyll Forest offers a new perspective on the National Park.

ARROCHAR AND LOCH LONG

Buses connect Arrochar with Glasgow, Dumbarton and Inveraray

Trains connect Arrochar with stations on the West Highland Railway

Information centre 📞 01301 702432

Lying on the shore of a sea loch, Arrochar has a contrasting feel to its close neighbour Tarbet, a mile to the east, and heralds a distinctive quarter of the National Park where the air is heavy with the smell of salt water and seaweed clings to the rocks on the shore. For over five centuries this area was held by the chiefs of Clan MacFarlane, but in 1784 their territory had to be sold to pay the debts of the 21st chief. The 25th, and last, clan chief died in 1866.

Arrochar has long had a coastal focus; in Victorian times steamers began plying the Clyde and, with its position on Long Long, Arrochar arrived on the tourist map. The Three Lochs Tour became a popular excursion, starting from Glasgow and taking in Loch Goil and Loch Long before travelling overland between Arrorchar and Tarbet, where a steamer could be caught to sail down Loch Lomond and join the railway at Balloch. The attraction of Arrochar as a staging post for the Arrochar Alps grew with the opening of the railway station as part of the West Highland Railway in 1894.

At the north end of the loch a path up Glen Loin leads to Loch Sloy and Inveruglas. The ash and oak woodlands on the north-west facing slopes of Cruach Tarbeirt are rich in woodland flowers. On the shores of Loch Long opposite Arrochar are the rusting remains of the **Arrochar Torpedo Testing Facility**, which provided work for the village for much of the twentieth century. Opened in 1912, it was used to test torpedoes made in nearby Greenock and Alexandria. Torpedoes were fired up Loch Long from tubes at the front of the facility. A boat stood by to recover the torpedoes and they were returned for analysis. The range's heyday was during the Second World War, when in 1944, more than 12,000 torpedoes were fired down the loch, working out at an average of 48 runs per day. The range closed in 1986 and is being dismantled.

Ardgartan Visitor Centre (☎ 08707 200606; www.forestry.gov. uk/scotland) at the mouth of Glen Croe offers access to walks and cycle routes through the Argyll Forest Park. The seasonal visitor centre has local tourism information and events and there is parking and toilets. The Forestry Commission Scotland also runs the nearby campsite. Three short walks and three cycle trails set out from the centre including the Ardgarten Peninsula Circuit, a tour of the wild rugged and remote Ardgartan peninsula, which is not accessible by car, and offers excellent views of the Clyde and the surrounding mountains.

The summit of the A83 along Glen Croe has for centuries been known as the **Rest and Be Thankful**. No doubt this is because this is what travellers would do after climbing from sea level to 270 metres in just 4 miles. However, the road is a recent addition over the pass. At first there was just a track made by generations of travellers and drovers taking herds of black cattle from Argyll to markets in the Lowlands. The

The commemorative stone at the Rest and Be Thankful

Jacobite uprisings were the impetus for road building in the Highlands and in 1743 it was decided to build 44 miles of military road from Dumbarton to Inveraray, via Loch Lomond, Tarbet, Arrochar, Glen Croe and down to Loch Fyne. A commemorative stone marking the completion of the road can be seen at the junction of the B828 and A83. It replaces the original, upon which the words 'Rest and Be Thankful' were carved and from which the pass gets its name. The climb up Glen Croe to Rest and Be Thankful is now the setting for an annual vintage car run.

THE ARROCHAR ALPS

The mountains clustered around Loch Long are among the best known in southern Scotland. Known as the Arrochar Alps, they have been a magnet for climbers and walkers for over 100 years. By the end of the nineteenth century the arrival of the railway had opened up the mountain around Loch Lomond to daytrippers from Glasgow. In 1899 William Naismith founded the Scottish Mountaineering Club and their journal over the next decade is littered with accounts of trips and climbs in the area. Although there are four Munros in the Arrochar Alps – Beinn Narnain, Ben Vane, Beinn Ime and Ben Vorlich – much of the attention in the early days was focused on a fifth summit, Ben

Arthur, more commonly known as the Cobbler. Its dramatic outline, carved by ice, frost and wind, can be seen from across Loch Long at Arrochar and beyond.

It was climbing on these crags which brought mountaineering to the area. The challenge of the Cobbler's triple peaks lures the best climbers of a generation and many people still travel here to test their skills on its crags. A traverse of the summit ridge is still seen as a classic climb. The origin of its name has puzzled many, including those early climbers and perhaps the best explanation is given by H.C. Boyd writing in the *Scottish Mountaineering Club Journal* in 1899:

> At this time of day it is almost superfluous to observe that the Cobbler boasts of three peaks – the North Peak, the Centre Peak, and the South Peak – all of them offering climbing of the most interesting nature, and of every shade of difficulty. Mr Maylard, in his reference to the popular nomenclature of the peaks, believes that the term 'Cobbler' is applied to the northern peak; but in this I think he is mistaken, and misses the whole significance of the name. In reality it is the central and highest peak that bears the name, and gives it to the whole mountain; and it does so on account of the very striking resemblance of the topmost blocks, as seen from Arrochar, to a little cowled figure sitting with his knees gathered up, like a cobbler bending over his work. The likeness is usually lost in a photograph, and is totally lost when seen from close at hand.
>
> He faces north, and over against him sits the ponderous and altogether disproportionate figure of 'the wife'. It is only her head and shoulders that we see – formed by the tremendous overhanging rocks of the northern peak – like an old woman in a mutch, stooping with age. Read Alexander Smith's description, in the 'Summer in Skye', of the domestic relations of this ancient couple, sitting for ever, in sunshine and in storm, unmoved and unchanged, brooding over the mystery of the years, and you can never afterwards look up at the quaint old outlines, sharply defined against the sky, without being impressed with a curiously vivid sense of personality. The south peak is popularly called 'The Cobbler's Last'. Among mountaineering men it is now rather familiarly known as 'Jean, the Cobbler's Lass'; and a shapely peak it is, a very pinnacle of pointed rock, springing from the depths of the corrie, on which side it is still perfectly virgin, and long will remain so. I have seen this pinnacle rising over the shoulder of Beinn Narnain, when half enshrouded in mist, look like some wonderful peak in the Dolomites, one might fancy miles away.

The most common approach to the Cobbler is from Loch Long; the path begins opposite the car park in Succoth. Once out of the forest, the path follows the glen between the Cobbler and Beinn Narnain. Shortly after the Narnain boulders the Cobbler path heads away left, while the

The Cobbler skyline, the signature of the Arrochar Alps

main glen track leads to paths up Beinn Ime and Beinn Narnain. Once on the summit ridge, the climb to the north peak is a scramble and should only be undertaken by experienced walkers or climbers. Descend by the same route.

Loch Goil

Buses connect Lochgoilhead and Castle Carrick with Dunoon

The B828 winds south from Rest and Be Thankful to the tranquil waters of Loch Goil, a 5-mile tongue of water which branches off Loch Long. It has historic associations with the Campbells as the Cowal peninsula was country which had to be crossed when travelling between Dunoon and the Lowlands and the clan stronghold at Inveraray. In the late nineteenth century horse-drawn carriages travelled twice a day from the head of Loch Goil and through **Hell's Glen** taking passengers to the Inveraray ferry at St Catherines. Hell's Glen is quieter today; the charcoal-burning fire which was once a common sight in its ancient oak woods, as in many of the glens of Cowal, has long since been extinguished. The only reminders of those days are the rectangular mileposts which punctuate the route to St Catherines.

Tranquil waters at Lochgoilhead

Lochgoilhead spreads comfortably around the top of the loch. It is a place for leisure; timeshare apartments perch on the glen sides, boats are moored on the water and walking, pony-trekking, fishing, sailing and canoeing can all be enjoyed here. Seals, otters, herons and seabirds also share the loch. The parish church contains the remains of a fourteenth-century medieval church, a present reminder of the clan past, as is the ornate monument to Sir James Campbell who died in 1592.

There is more Campbell history a further 5 miles down the loch at **Castle Carrick**, where the remains of a fortress stand against the

Castle Carrick

foreshore. The rectangular stronghold was built for the Campbells at the end of the fourteenth century. Its defence was originally secured by a deep moat with a drawbridge so that the castle was completely surrounded by sea. It had a large hall on the first floor and was used as a royal hunting lodge by James IV during the fifteenth century when wild boar used to roam the surrounding hills. It was burned down by government forces in 1685 following the rebellion of the 9th Earl of Argyll, who was subsequently executed for treason. These were unforgiving times.

The Cowal Way

www.cowalway.com

The Cowal Way is an unofficial 57-mile long-distance path which begins on the shore of Loch Fyne and traverses the Cowal peninsula to Loch Long. From there it passes the Cobbler – that can be climbed as an excursion – before heading up Glen Loin to finish at Inveruglas. It runs in quiet and often remote and rugged countryside, with fine views over Bute and the Firth of Clyde, lochside and woodland walking, prehistoric heritage and interesting wildlife.

Glenbranter

www.forestry.gov.uk/scotland

The National Park boundary does not extend as far as Loch Fyne, so to visit the National Park south of Glen Kinglas continue along the A815 Loch Fyne road and re-enter the National Park south of Strachur. This route passes St Catherines, where ferries once sailed across Loch Fyne to Inveraray, and **Ardkinglas House and Gardens**. Designed by architect Sir Robert Lorimer and built in 1907, the house and gardens are open to the public.

The leasing of **Glenbranter Forest** from Scottish comedian Sir Harry Lauder in 1921 marked the start of the Forestry Commission Scotland's work in Cowal. A memorial to his son who was killed during the First World War stands on the east side of the A815 after the Glenbranter Forest turning. The hamlet was built for forest workers in the 1950s. Behind the houses, the car park stands on the site of the original Glenbranter House. This is the start of the three Lauder Forest walks and three cycle routes: two circular routes and one which contours the shores

Loch Eck has high conservation value because of its unusual fish population

of Loch Eck to Benmore Botanic Garden. The Forestry Commission Scotland also runs events from Glenbranter.

Loch Eck

There are several picnic spots on the 7 miles of shore between Glenbranter and Benmore Botanic Garden, good places from which to enjoy this unique loch. The legend of the loch is that it was formed following a tragic accident. One harvest time, when the valley was filled with local reapers, the Cailleach Bhear, a well-known Celtic mountain nymph, sent her servant Balach to a nearby sacred well for water. Unfortunately he forgot to close the magic tap and a flood engulfed the valley.

In 1780 a flash flood did sweep through the valley, but no lives were lost. The real flood happened after the last ice age when sea water inundated the ice-carved glen. As the land rose it left behind a strange mixture of freshwater and seawater fish which slowly adapted to the loch. Now it has one of the most distinctive fish communities in Britain. Along with Loch Lomond it is one of only two places in Scotland where the herring-like powan live. The loch is also home to Arctic char, salmon and sea trout, making Loch Eck the only place in Britain where these four species occur together. Special care is now being taken to conserve the loch.

For many years it was Loch Eck and not the adjacent road that was the transport link between Dunoon and Loch Fyne. Steamers sailed the loch for nearly a century from the 1820s to the First World War. In the 1880s Loch Eck was part of a tour which operated between Glasgow and Edinburgh, Dunoon, Inveraray and Bute. The last steamer ran in 1926 and the remains of the pier can still be seen at the head of the loch

Benmore Botanic Garden

Garden open 1 March – 31 October; café and shop open all year.

📞 01369 706261; **www.rbge.org.uk/benmore**

Buses connect Benmore Botanic Garden with Dunoon

First Scotrail offers an all-inclusive Benmore Botanic Garden Day Out ticket within Strathclyde, including train to Gourock, ferry to Dunoon and bus to Benmore, plus admission to the Garden 📞 08457 550033

West Coast Motors also offers an all-inclusive ticket including bus fare and admission 📞 01586 550139

Benmore Botanic Garden, in the dramatic woodland setting of the Strath Eachaig, is home to some of the tallest trees in Britain. The mild climate makes ideal growing conditions for the unusual plants and flowers found here. The Garden has nearly 5,000 different species including over 300 types of rhododendron and one third of the world's coniferous trees which have been collected from around the globe, making a walk in the Garden a unique experience within the National Park.

Between 1904 and 1932 George Forrest collected more than 30,000 plant specimens and more than 100,000 seeds in western China for the Royal Botanic Garden Edinburgh. A search was started for a home for the collection and in the 1920s they were brought to Benmore, which was already well stocked with exotic trees and shrubs. In 1863 an avenue of giant redwoods was planted which are now more than 50 metres tall. Research, conservation and education remain an important focus for the Garden and in 1995 a small area was cleared to recreate a Chilean rainforest with plants like the monkey puzzle tree, southern beech and bamboo. An intriguing addition to the landscape, the Garden also helps to conserve plants that are under threat around the world.

The Garden has more than 6 miles of footpaths and you can also use it as a starting point for a longer walk exploring the river Eachaig. A short distance up Glen Massan brings you to Stone Cottage, where there is parking and from where a path leads to the summit of Ben More after which the Garden is named. The path is suitable for experienced walkers only.

The exotic colours of Benmore Botanic Garden

Kilmun and the Cowal Coast

The Cowal coast is the National Park's marine gateway. As the river Eachaig winds its way from Loch Eck into Holy Loch, tonnes of silt washed down from the mountain form deep mudflats, a far cry from the heights of the Munros further inland. Here wading birds like curlews, redshanks and oystercatchers probe the mud for worms and overturn stones in search of crabs and insects. The smell of the sea and the rhythm of the tide reinforce the sense of the coast as the dominant natural force in this part of the National Park.

 Kilmun Arboretum (2 miles; easy)

There are more woodland walks at **Kilmun Arboretum**. Short waymarked routes mean you can discover more about this fascinating research woodland. It was chosen in the 1930s by the Forestry Commission as a test ground for planting species of tree from around the world to see which would thrive in the UK's damp climate. Over the next 50 years nearly 300 different species were planted and monitored. There are now more than 160 types of tree planted in groups or mini forests. In 1991 the Royal Botanic Garden Edinburgh, which also manages Benmore Botanic Garden 3 miles to the north, began a project at Kilmun to conserve threatened conifer species and create a seed bank for new growth elsewhere.

Puck's Glen (2 miles; moderate)

Walking through the magical Puck's Glen

One mile south of Benmore Botanic Garden are the Forestry Commission Scotland walks at **Puck's Glen**. There are three walks of different lengths but the highlight is the path up Puck's Glen – one of the most well-known routes in the Argyll Forest. From the car park a path leads into the glen. Countless waterfalls, lush vegetation and the continuous sound of water dripping from rocks and rushing through the glen combine to provide the walk with the atmosphere of a rainforest.

The village of **Kilmun** has a long association with Holy Loch, on whose banks it stands. Tradition associates its name with St Mun, a follower of St Columba, who reputedly built a place of worship on its shores when he landed here in the sixth century. Kilmun is a Gaelic name – 'the church of St Mun' – reflecting the place where St Mun planted the first seeds of Christianity in the area. For thirty years of the Cold War, Holy Loch was a United States Navy submarine base,

Oystercatcher

with 4,000 US navy personnel, civilians and dependants based here and making up one third of the population. Their departure in the early 1990s has left the Cowal coast a quieter place although the military presence has not disappeared completely: outside the National Park on the eastern shore of Loch Long is the Trident submarine base at Coulport.

One of the most interesting places to visit in the village is **Kilmun Church**. Although the present church was built in 1841, the original building was founded in 1442 by Sir Duncan Campbell. He is buried here and you can see his effigy in the church. Clad in plate armour, the detail of his clothing and weaponry is still well preserved. Many of the Campbell clan have been buried in a square mausoleum in the churchyard, including the Marquis of Argyll, who was executed for treason in 1661. Although his body came to Kilmun soon after his death, his severed head was exhibited around the kingdom as a warning to others and it was three more years before body and head were reunited.

Unusually, Kilmun Church was a collegiate church: a church with an associated clergy. That it was the only one in the Highlands was a measure of its significance. The squat ivy-covered tower next to the church is all that remains of the original building and was where the clergy lived and slept.

It was also the site of one of the bloodiest conflicts of the clan era on the Cowal, between Clan Campbell and their neighbours Clan

Kilmun Church, with its medieval tower in the graveyard

Lamont whose strongholds were castles at Toward and Ascog west of Dunoon. The two clans were never on the best of terms and feuds and fighting were a way of life. But things took a downturn in 1646 when Sir James Lamont joined forces with the mercenary soldier Alistair MacColla. Together they descended on the Campbell lands in north Cowal, killing and burning men, woman, children, cattle and crops. When they came to Kilmun, the story goes that the invaders attacked the tower. Once those inside the tower had surrendered under promise of their lives being spared, the prisoners were then taken 3 miles away and put to death.

Unsurprisingly the Campbells didn't take too kindly to the ravaging of their lands. Within months they laid siege to the Lamonts' castles at Toward and Ascog and finally the garrisons agreed to surrender provided they were given safe passage. The Campbells agreed. However, no sooner had they laid down their weapons than Lamont strongholds were looted and burnt to the ground and prisoners were shipped off to Dunoon by boat. At the churchyard about 100 Lamonts, including women and children, were shot or stabbed to death. Thirty-six of the clan's high-ranking gentlemen were hanged from a tree in the churchyard, cut down and then buried either dead or alive in a common grave. There is a memorial to those killed in Dunoon.

The pier at Kilmun, which is now disused, was a regular port of call for steamers up until its closure in 1971. Presently the only marine access to the National Park is now at **Blairmore** where a local heritage trust

The coast at Ardentinny

(www.blairmoreheritage.com) has restored the 150-year-old pier and built a small visitor centre.

The last stop on the National Park coast is at **Ardentinny**. Forestry is the focus of this small hamlet, which also offers the novel prospect of relaxing on one of the few stretches of sandy beach on the Cowal coast at the Forestry Commission Scotland picnic area. There is no road access north of Ardentinny until Castle Carrick, on what is one of the wildest stretches of coastland in the National Park.

Acknowledgements

The author would like to especially thank Hannah Stirling for her contribution towards the publication of this guide. Thanks also go to the Loch Lomond & The Trossachs National Park Authority for its support, in particular Sheila Winstone for her help in providing maps, photographs and encouragement. Additional thanks go to Esther Smith, George Boyd and John Digney who helped with proof-reading and Andrew Simmons at Birlinn who helped make the book a reality.

Picture Credits

Index